CHINA
IN
CHANGE

6 China, Canada and the United States: A Canadian Perspective

E. Bruce Copland

THIS CHAPTER will deal with the complex and baffling problems of the recent and current relations between North America and China. It is necessary first, however, to give a brief account of the relations of the United States and Canada with China before 1949.

RELATIONS BEFORE 1949

First, the relations of both countries with China were moderately satisfactory up to the end of World War II, though at times some issues caused friction and resentment. Second, the American relationship has been of longer duration and of much greater importance, to China and the United States, than that of Canada. Third, since 1949 there have been more differences in the relations of the United States with China, and Canada with China, than in any previous period.

United States contacts with China began at the end of the eighteenth century. These contacts increased steadily, though somewhat haphazardly. The initiative was entirely on the American side and involved trade, promotion of U. S. interests and missionary work.

One important aspect of U. S.-China relations has been noted by many writers—the emotional involvement of Americans. From the beginning, Americans have had deep feelings about China, while in Canada there has never been the same intensity of emotional involvement. This is not true wholly because of Canada's smaller effort. It is partly a matter of difference in national temperaments. Canadians are cautious in making commitments. They have never been as greatly involved in Chinese affairs, and have not been so disillusioned when matters have gone wrong.

The United States China trade began in 1784, and in 1844 the first Sino-American treaty was peacefully negotiated. In the case of Canada, trade with China began late in the nineteenth century. From 1890, the Canadian Pacific ships were well known in the Far East. The volume of trade with China, and the number of Chinese immigrants wanting to enter Canada, resulted in the stationing at Hong Kong and Shanghai of Canadian trade commissioners and immigration officers. Canadians living in China were registered with the British consulates for whatever jurisdiction was necessary. In 1943 the first Canadian ambassador arrived in the wartime capital of Chungking. Canadian diplomatic personnel remained in Nanking until 1951.

Missionaries from the U. S. began work in China early in the nineteenth century, and their numbers continued to grow until 1925. Canadian Protestant work in China began, in 1872, in Taiwan, and there were also large groups of missionaries in various sections of mainland China. Canadian Roman Catholic mission work began in the twentieth century, in Manchuria and some other areas.

Up to World War II a large part of the information about China that was available to the general public in North America was furnished by missionaries, in addresses given when they were on furlough, in letters, in articles for missionary and other publications and in books. During this period, there were no significant differences in emphasis between what was reported by U. S. and Canadian missionaries.

There was a change in the relations of China with North America in the early years of the twentieth century. Before 1900, Chinese intellectuals had made an attempt to bring about constitutional reform, and the Boxer Uprising in 1900 was the last reaction of the Manchus against internal reform and Western influences. When the Chinese government decided in 1905 to adopt the Western type of curriculum, foreign teachers were sought and welcomed, rather than tolerated as they had been in the past. The numbers of Protestant missionaries increased greatly in the years from 1900 to 1925.

In North America the overthrow of the Manchus and the efforts of Sun Yat-sen to establish a republic in China were welcomed sympathetically. After the death of Dr. Sun in 1925 and the rise to power of Chiang Kai-shek, people in both the U. S. and Canada showed great interest in the welfare of Nationalist China. Knowledge about China was increasing constantly. Many of Chiang's officials, trained abroad, were trying to apply Western techniques to the modernization of China.

It was during World War II that political relationships with China became extremely important, and also very difficult, for the United States. American newsmen and diplomats in Chungking were well aware of the acute struggle between the Kuomintang and the Communists. They also sensed the constant friction between the American army men and the Chinese military and government officials. Foreigners who visited the Chinese Communist headquarters at Yenan usually came away with a favorable impression.

The American public at the end of the war had little idea about the strength of Chinese communism. It did not adequately realize, and even now does not, that communism in China began to develop as early as 1919 and that the party was founded in 1921. Even though the Chinese Communists were few in number, and constantly in danger of their lives at the hands of Chiang's troops and agents after 1927, they were always able to maintain control over *some* areas in China. The Communist armies were trained in guerrilla tactics, and they protected the areas that their civil officials administered. Thus, by the time the Communists gained control of China in 1949, they had a trained and seasoned army and a strong nucleus of civil officials. The Communist take-over in Peking in 1949 was thus no sudden victory but one for which they had had long and disciplined preparation.

One of the extremely few foreigners who worked with the Communists in the hard wilderness years was Dr. Norman Bethune, a famous Canadian surgeon. During the Spanish Civil War Bethune had set up a remarkable blood transfusion service. Early in 1938 he became convinced that the Chinese Communists needed medical help even more than his Spanish republican friends, and he worked with unbelievable energy and devotion to provide medical service for the Communist armies. His aim was to treat the wounded close to the combat areas, and to train Chinese medical aides to do this work. Bethune died of septicemia in November, 1939, already a hero among Chinese Communists. To every Chinese school child, Canada is Bethune's country. For mass education in the Cultural Revolution, Mao Tse-tung published (1967) a small volume of three earlier essays extolling models of Communist commitment. Remarkably, one was his eulogy of a foreigner, a Westerner, Dr. Bethune.

When the fighting came to an end in World War II, the primary aim of most Americans was to "get the boys home." In China there was danger of civil war between the Kuomintang and the Communists, and General Marshall was appointed to try to mediate between Chiang and the Communists. Even with Marshall's great prestige and ability, his mission was doomed to failure. Chiang was never willing to negotiate with the Communists, and the Communists believed, with reason, that they were sure to win. Marshall's frustration was shared by most Americans who were interested in China's welfare and in Sino-American friendship. A vocal minority in the United States advocated full American military support for Chiang against the Communists. Not a few Americans still imagine that the Chinese Communists could have been defeated at that time if adequate financial and military backing had been given to Chiang.

A description of how things looked to a responsible Canadian observer, written in August, 1947, when American policy appeared to be in formulation, has now become available for our examination:

Since the end of the war, the effect of American policy, whatever its intention, has been to bolster up the Nanking government. The question now in the minds of all Chinese, and many others, is—What will America do next? We may assume that the United States does not intend to withdraw from China. How, then, will American power operate? It may be that the United States government has already decided that whatever is done in China must be part of a plan to oppose or stop Russia. If this is so, and recent news from the United States indicates that hysterical anti-Russian sentiment is dominant, then probably the United States will give military and economic aid to Chiang without any conditions. Such a course of action is understandable but it will increase internal bitterness in China, and will antagonize Chinese liberals still more, and alienate them from the country which in the past they have regarded as the home of democracy and to a large extent their spiritual home.

These observations give some idea of the gravity of the situation in 1947. They reflect the involvement of the United States government in Chinese affairs and its strong desire to support Chiang's stand against the Communists. On this point, there was considerable difference of opinion between American and Canadian diplomatic personnel in China. Canada's diplomats were unanimous in their disapproval of the Kuomintang, though they were not pro-Communist. The Canadian point of view is well put by John Holmes: "Canadians had been neither personally nor emotionally engaged in the postwar effort to bolster the Kuomintang, and there was none of the feeling of having 'lost China' which deeply affected American thinking." [1]

The Dominant United States Stance

When the Communist government was established in Peking, the U. S. government was rather disillusioned over postwar developments in China. Officials were reluctant to take on any more responsibility in Asia, and at the same time did not possess sufficient understanding of the strength and determination of the new Peking government. In these circumstances, Washington adopted a wait-and-see attitude; meanwhile, relations with Chiang's refugee regime on Taiwan were maintained. It seems clear that during the winter and spring of 1949-1950, the American government would not have used its armed forces to prevent the Communists' taking over Taiwan. At that time, Taiwan was not regarded, as it was later, as being essential in the chain of United States strong points in East Asia. In this same period the Canadian Department of External Affairs was preparing to recognize the government in Peking at an opportune time. The opportune time did not come, and has not come yet. The event that put off Canadian recognition of the People's Republic, and made American recognition unthinkable for years to come, was the Korean War.

Every careful study of the relations between North America and China during the past twenty years shows that decisions made by the American government at the beginning of the Korean War have influenced policy and thinking ever since. The North Korean attack on South Korea in June, 1950, was a challenge to American security and prestige. The matter was brought to the United Nations, which decided that the attack constituted aggression and the defense of South Korea was a United Nations enterprise in which U. S. forces took the major share. Many well-informed American authorities did not expect Communist China to intervene in the Korean conflict. Peking's intervention, and the humiliation of American forces defeated by Chinese troops in North Korea, did more to harden American attitudes against Chinese communism than anything that had happened up to that time. Although there had been growing apprehension in the United States about events in China from the end of World War II until the establishment of the Communist government in 1949, there was still a reservoir of goodwill toward China. The Communist actions against U. S. troops in Korea resulted in general American anger against China, and not a little fear of China's new power. In spite of all that happened in Korea and the anti-American propaganda from Peking, however, many Americans in the missionary constituency, and some others, continued to have a high regard for the Chinese people.

Although token forces of Canadian troops went to the aid of South Korea in 1950, Canada's involvement with China has been on an extremely limited scale. Negotiations looking toward recognition of Peking were resumed in 1954, and the matter was again considered by the Canadian government in 1956 and 1957. In Canada, there was no emotional block to calm consideration of this issue. It could be looked at like any other matter affecting national interest, with the usual Canadian caution and an ear to the ground in the direction of Washington.

It was the confrontation of the United States and China during the Korean War that expanded the U. S. involvement in Asia. Japan's defeat had left a power vacuum in the Pacific around Japan, Korea, Okinawa and Taiwan. This was filled in by the American navy. Up to the time of the Korean War, American anxiety centered in the Russian alliance with China and the threat of international communism. In the Korean War, China was seen to be a new menace in Asia, calling for the American policy of containment.

In June, 1950, President Harry S. Truman gave orders for the Seventh Fleet to neutralize the Taiwan Strait. Most present-day American-Chinese problems stem from this decision. The fact that the Communists were prevented from attacking Taiwan meant that Chiang Kai-shek could consolidate his strength there, with the assurance of American protection and support. His government has been recognized since 1950 as the government of China, with the right to Chinese representation in the United Nations and a seat on the Security Council. This support of Chiang's government, and the defense of Taiwan, have been since 1950 foundation stones in the American policy to contain China.

An increasing number of thoughtful Americans have been unhappy in recent years about the inflexibility of this policy. But at least three factors operate to make drastic modification extremely difficult. First, there is the inflexibility of Peking. The Communist government there has controlled all China except Taiwan since 1949-1950. It regards Taiwan as part of China, and everything related to Taiwan as a domestic matter in which foreign powers should not meddle. Second, there is the present involvement of the United States in Vietnam; until that issue is settled the United States is unlikely to modify its China policy. Finally, there is Chiang Kai-shek. So long as he is living, and head of the government in Taiwan, it seems certain that the United States would not go back on its 1954 mutual defense pact with him.

In spite of all the obstacles to working out a new China policy, which would be in accord with present realities in China and the Far East, many thoughtful Americans favor effort in that direction. Robert Blum has stated his convictions:

We cannot be sure that efforts to reach a reasonable understanding with the Chinese Communists will succeed. The current prospects are not good. The present commitment of the Chinese leaders to a hostile attitude toward the United States is strong and will not easily be changed. But we must try. Until we take the initiative, affirm our leadership, and pursue our goals more vigorously but with greater prudence, patience, and understanding, we cannot know whether or not, over time, a better basis of relations, or at least a reduction in the present level of tension and hostility, can be achieved.[2]

We are still left with the thorny problem of the future of Taiwan and its 13,000,000 people. Such peace as the people of Taiwan enjoy is due to the power of the American Seventh Fleet. The present prosperity of Taiwan is due to the industry and ability of the people of Chinese ancestry who live on the island, the sound economic foundations in agriculture and industry laid by the Japanese colonial administration, the abundant natural resources and temperate climate, good economic planning by the present government and the wise use of American economic aid in recent years.

What do the Taiwanese themselves want? What should they have under present circumstances? The first need is to understand just who the Taiwanese, who constitute some 85 percent of the population, are. They are the descendants of settlers from South Fukien who migrated to Taiwan in the seventeenth and eighteenth centuries. They spoke the Amoy dialect, which is still their mother tongue. The Japanese never prevented them from using their own language at home, in social life and in business—nor has the present government in Taiwan. Under Japan,

CHINA, CANADA AND THE U.S. 155

Japanese was the language taught in school and required in all official business. Since Taiwan was returned to China in 1945, Mandarin has been the language taught in school and required for official business.

It is essential to understand that all adult Taiwanese think of themselves as Taiwanese and *not* as Chinese, except in a racial and to some degree in a cultural sense. Taiwan is their only home. A "return" to mainland China means nothing to a Taiwanese—he himself has never been there and has no interests or stake there.

The people of Taiwan welcomed the representatives of the government of the Republic of China when they arrived in 1945 and 1946. But they soon discovered that long separation from the mainland during fifty years of Japanese rule had brought them a differing cultural and social character, with the result that under Nationalist rule there have been times of tension and bitterness. On the whole, the Taiwanese have merely tolerated the present government.

The constant propaganda of the Chiang government is that all who live in Taiwan are Chinese and that they are happy under Nationalist rule. Many foreigners who live in Taiwan accept this contention, but it cannot be substantiated.

The Taiwanese would like to have self-government. What they *can* have is another matter. They have had almost no experience in administration except in local government. Taiwan has a large population, however, and is a viable economic entity; its people are well educated, industrious and competent; it could be a national state if given a chance.

Since 85 percent of the people on the island are Taiwanese, and since Taiwan is their only home, they should be given a responsible share in any decisions regarding their future. The writer has the strong impression that the United States government, because almost all its relations are with Chiang's officials, has never given adequate consideration to the Taiwanese point of view.

The Meaning of the Canadian Experience

We turn to Canadian relations with China, which are intertwined with the total relationship between Canada and the United States. Beyond the intrinsic importance of these subjects, we will try to suggest to Americans how attitudes in the United States toward China may damage —indeed, have damaged—the standing and influence of the United States in relationships with countries less congenial than Canada. Understanding and cooperation from others require a mutuality which the United States has not steadily manifested in this difficult area of policy toward China, where national interests and judgments diverge. We do not imply that Canadians and others of comparable views are right and Americans wrong. We do mean that more openness on the part of the United States to informed opinion on China in Canada and other friendly

CHINA, CANADA AND THE U.S.

countries can benefit both the U. S. and the entire world.

When in June, 1950, North Korea attacked the South, Canada took an active part in the decisions and actions of the United Nations. In the period of the Korean War, Canadian forces participated in the effort to halt aggression. At the same time, Canada maintained a moderate attitude toward Communist China. There was a new and positive Canadian effort in these years to work through the Commonwealth in establishing relations with democratic nations in Asia. Canada has made considerable contributions, in personnel and in finance, to the Colombo Plan, and this has brought a number of intelligent Canadians into close contact with several non-Communist Asian nations. It has made Canadians sympathetic with Asian aspirations, economic and political. At the same time it has made Canadians apprehensive of, and opposed to, the apparently wholehearted American support of the Chiang regime in Formosa, Diem and successors in South Vietnam, Syngman Rhee and successors in South Korea. Well-informed Canadians have known that the issues were very complicated and that United States responsibility and power in Asia involves making decisions that Canada did not have to make.

Canada has not recognized the Peking government, but the matter has been reviewed from time to time with varying degrees of urgency. Despite the lack of formal relationships, a fair number of important contacts have been maintained through Canadians who have visited China or resided there. Able Canadian journalists living in Peking have provided information valued not only by Canadian papers but also by United States media, which largely depend for news on China watchers in Hong Kong.

Trade has been increasingly important in the Canadian attitude toward China. Canadian trade commissioners are in constant touch with China through dealings with Chinese agents in Hong Kong and periodic visits to several large cities in China. Until 1960 Canada's trade with China, sales and purchases, balanced at about $5,000,000 a year. But in the years since 1961 China's purchases of Canadian wheat have been between $100,000,000 and $150,000,000 a year. There has been considerable criticism in the United States of Canada's trade with China. Canada answers that it is not right to withhold food supplies from people because of disapproval of their government's policy. On a pragmatic basis, foreign trade is much more vital to Canada than to the United States. Canadian wheat sales may soon diminish or cease, but they have probably been the decisive factor in creating what at least seems to be a majority opinion in Canada favoring the recognition of Peking.

Canadian policy in regard to relations with China may have been lacking in clarity and decisiveness. In regard to this, John Holmes makes an important comment:

> . . . It reflects a recognition that it is American rather than Canadian policy which matters, a suspicion that an independent Canadian gesture would be futile and perhaps pretentious unless it could conceivably affect the American position of the disposition of the U.N. General Assembly. The dilemma of the Canadian government is that Canada's China policy is inextricably involved with Canada's general relation with the United States. . . .
> Canada has the obligations of a lesser to a major ally, obligations for which there is no ready-made formula.[3]

Canadians are unhappy about the Vietnam war. In a general way Canada approves the American aim to maintain order in Southeast Asia, though not some of the methods used. Some Canadian firms are profiting by the sale of war materials to the United States for use in Vietnam. And in the complex situation that prevails, with American soldiers being killed daily, Canada is not likely to do more than express strong disapproval of American military actions.

The differences in American and Canadian policy toward China can only be properly understood in the overall context of Canadian-American relations, which for a hundred years have been uniquely good. The problems that do arise pertain to the existence of a small nation next to a super-power. A favorite word used in the most constructive of recent writings on Canadian-American relations is "partnership." But it is a partnership between a small nation and a super-power. The small nation *is* a nation, with a national consciousness deep and cherished, even while it is struggling to attain its true identity. From time to time political or economic decisions are made in the United States, on matters touching vital Canadian interests, without prior, or at any rate adequate, consultation with Canada. In such situations Canadian emotions are aroused, and feelings are crucial in personal and international relations. The real issue is how a partnership between a powerful and a weak partner can be made to work. Wisely, the Department of State has recently established a new Bureau of Canadian Affairs, under a senior officer. Its main purpose is to avoid situations in which American decisions are taken without awareness of their implications for Canada.

Competent American students of the Canadian-American relationship warn that unless the United States is very careful, the national identity that Canada is seeking will, in economic aspects, "be built around the principle of anti-Americanism." They say of the central issue, "the underlying feature of all Canadian foreign policy is that seldom, if ever, is Ottawa willing to take any decision that it suspects may aggravate Washington. If Canadian foreign policy is written in Washington it cannot serve Canadian interests ideally, or American interests either. . . . Partnership between Canada and the

CHINA, CANADA AND THE U.S.

United States cannot be possible or productive unless Canada has an independent foreign policy in which agreement with the United States is a matter of choice, not a matter of power."[4]

Finally, the impressive appeal of the career diplomat A. D. P. Heeney, twice Canada's ambassador in Washington, stresses the moral and practical obligation of the United States. Continuation of satisfactory relationships depends on the actual *behavior* of the two governments and peoples toward one another.

We cannot reply solely upon the negative inter-dependence arising from our geography, our history or our economic and social involvement with one another. And here the greater, more onerous responsibility—because of the disproportion in power and influence between the two—seems to me clearly to rest on the shoulders of the United States, that is to say if it wishes to have alongside it a self-respecting ally and a partner rather than a nagging reluctant satellite.[5]

Christian Attitudes, 1949–1968

When the Communist government was established in 1949, most Christian people in North America were disappointed or hostile. Those who supported missionary work in China were concerned about the safety of missionaries; they wondered whether the church in China could continue its worship and its witness. As the withdrawal of missionaries proceeded from 1949 to 1951, it became clear that individual missionaries knew only what they had been able to observe, usually in circumstances where their freedom of movement was much restricted. The wisest observers were reluctant to make judgments about general conditions or future trends. Meanwhile, the Korean War occupied the public mind, and hostility to the Chinese Communists increased markedly in the United States and to some extent in Canada. Before the Korean War had ended, and for the next several years, public opinion in the United States was influenced and poisoned by Senator Joseph McCarthy and those who agreed or sympathized with him. It was dangerous to be considered in any degree pro-Communist in those years. In spite of the inhospitable atmosphere, studies on Christianity and communism were carried on under the auspices of the National Council of Churches in the 1950's. In 1958 the Cleveland World Order Study Conference advocated modification of American China policy and consideration of the admission of China to the United Nations.

For the past ten years, church committees on international affairs have continued to study the China question. Many statements have been issued, always emphasizing that for the attainment of world understanding and peace, China must be represented in international consultations pertaining to Asia, and to the world. One of the most important, and pertinent, of all church statements on the China question was that approved by the General Board of the National Council of Churches of Christ in the USA on February 22, 1966. The vote was 90 in favor, 3 against and 1 abstaining. The preamble and the four most important sections are:

Opening the way for full participation by the People's Republic of China within the framework of international institutions and diplomatic intercourse presents many complicated problems, but we believe it is essential that further steps be taken for improving relationships with a people who comprise nearly one-fourth of the human race. . . . Even while recognizing the increasing belligerence of the mainland China government, we, as Christians, and therefore as witnesses to a Lord who reconciles us all, recommend the following actions: . . .

2. That the United States, without prejudice to its own policy concerning diplomatic recognition, and under conditions which take into account the welfare, security and political status of Taiwan, including membership in the United Nations, develop a new policy of support to the seating of the People's Republic of China in the United Nations;

3. That careful study be given by the United States to regularizing diplomatic communication with the People's Republic of China and to the conditions under which diplomatic recognition may appropriately be extended; . . .

5. That the United States should publicly and unilaterally take steps in the direction of free travel between the United States and mainland China; . . .

8. That every effort be made to involve the People's Republic of China in international negotiations

regarding such issues as disarmament, non-proliferation of nuclear weapons, and a nuclear test ban.

The sections not quoted had to do with the establishment of a presidential commission on American China policy, church efforts to open communications with Chinese Christians, sale of food and nonstrategic materials to China, arrangements for cultural exchanges and possible technical cooperation.

On February 21, 1968, the General Board of the National Council adopted another policy statement on China, within a document of global range on "Imperatives of Peace and Responsibilities of Power." The vote on this occasion was 100 in favor and 14 opposed. The chief paragraphs concerning China provided that the U. S., recognizing the need to achieve a stability that would reassure China's weak neighbors, should acknowledge the fact that China has legitimate interests in Asia and that she will exert a significant influence in that region. The statement went on:

Instead of trying to isolate the People's Republic of China, the U. S. should take positive steps to bring it, if possible, into the international community. While maintaining awareness that many policies of the Government of the People's Republic of China fosters self-isolation, the United States should take the initiative, unilaterally if necessary, for developing contacts in travel and cultural exchange; it should open the possibility of trade in non-strategic items; it should espouse an honorable formula for seating the

People's Republic of China in the United Nations while retaining a seat for Taiwan.

A number of American churches have adopted resolutions during the past three years, in most cases broadly similar to the National Council statements. Among the most comprehensive of these are the statements adopted by the General Assembly of the United Presbyterian Church in 1966 and 1967 and those made by the Methodists and the Disciples of Christ.

In 1966 the Central Conference of American Rabbis made a statement on international affairs, which included these sentences:

. . . we recognize that the isolation of mainland China, whether self-imposed or enforced from outside, bodes ill for the future of mankind. We re-affirm our previous Conference position on the advisability of universality of membership in the United Nations, and we urge our government and the government of Canada actively to support the seating of the People's Republic of China in the United Nations. We commend our national administration for the efforts it has made to foster that change in economic and cultural relations that may pierce the barrier separating us from the Chinese People's Republic and may persuade mainland China to accept its place in the community of nations should a tender be made to it.

The most recent World Council of Churches resolution on China, reiterating a position taken earlier as part of longer statements, was adopted by the Central Committee in Geneva in February, 1966. The section on China reads:

That every effort be made to bring the 700 million people of China, through the Government in power, The People's Republic of China, into the world community of nations in order that they may assume their reasonable responsibility and avail themselves of legitimate opportunity to provide an essential ingredient for peace and security not only in Southeast Asia, but throughout the entire world.

All these statements have been carefully and responsibly drawn up by people well informed about international affairs, and about China. The statements reflect a deep desire for communication with the Chinese people, especially with Chinese fellow-Christians, and a concern for reconciliation between the United States and China. Not by any means all church members, or American citizens, or government officials approved these statements, but they have been formulated by Christians who believe in making known their convictions about the relations between the United States and China. It must be remembered, however, that Peking would not now consent to establish relations with Washington, or to be a member of the United Nations, on the basis proposed in these statements.

There have been some differences in the Christian attitudes to the China question between the United States and Canada, partly because the United States is much more deeply involved but also because Canadians were not hindered by McCarthyism in the 1950's.

CHINA, CANADA AND THE U.S.

Among Canadian churches, the one that has the most active committee on international affairs, and that has urged action most frequently on the Canadian government, is the United Church of Canada. This church at its General Council (national assembly) in 1966 "reaffirmed the conviction first expressed in 1952 and again in 1956, 1958, 1960 and 1964 that the Government of Canada should give recognition, without further delay, to the Government of the People's Republic of China."

No other Canadian church has taken so strong or so consistent a position in regard to relations with China. Some churches, notably the Roman Catholic Church, have taken no action. Lack of unanimity about the larger China issues has prevented the Canadian Council of Churches from taking action parallel to that of the National Council of Churches in the USA and the World Council of Churches.

At the March, 1968, meeting of the General Board of Missions of the Presbyterian Church in Canada an important statement was approved, entitled "Our Concern for the People of Continental China." [10] The position of the Presbyterian Church in Canada has particular interest because of its historic Christian effort both in China and in Taiwan. Indeed, no other Christian body in North America has exactly this experience and situation. Current circumstances limit to Taiwan its mission to people of Chinese race. But this church refuses to be confined by political limitations, or to be restrictively prejudiced by its living ties with the people of Taiwan. The statement adopted reaffirms an abiding concern for all Chinese people, and urges upon the Presbyterian Church in Canada a number of specific measures looking to the increase of knowledge and understanding concerning China, in the church constituency and in the Canadian nation through encouragement of study, contact, trade and cultural exchanges.

The Christian faith is a faith for the world. Christian missionaries went to China to share with people there a knowledge of Jesus Christ who is "the way, and the truth, and the life." Whatever was done in the past in China by Christians, with pure motives and loving concern, despite human weakness and errors, which should be recognized, was part of God's work in the world. It was not mistaken or unfruitful effort, "down the drain," as many people now claim.

At present, personal contacts between people in the Western world and those in mainland China are few, and meaningful communication is difficult. But the way of communication through prayer is never closed to Christians who have faith, knowledge of how to pray in these circumstances, and persistence.

The hope for establishing personal relationships between Christians in North America and China in the foreseeable future is dim. In these circumstances, how can we cultivate a right attitude toward China and the Chinese people? It can only be possible through genuine concern, considerable knowledge about China and above all through the use of imagination.

The people of the United States and Canada live on the same continent and enjoy excellent relationships. But Canadians are annoyed by the common U. S. assumption that what is good for the United States must be good for Canada. Canadians, like the people of every nation, have a justifiable national pride. If it is hard for Americans to remember that Canadians are different, and have a different way of looking at things, and that Canadian national interest is not always the same as that of the United States, how much *more* difficult will it be for Americans to try to understand the Chinese point of view?

It is doubtful whether any non-Chinese can ever fully understand the Chinese way of thinking. But now, more than ever, it is important for Americans *to try* to understand the Chinese point of view. This does not mean that we must agree with Chinese claims or policy. Chinese national interest can never be the same as American national interest. But we must indicate, through any channel of communication open to us, that we are ready to listen to whatever the Chinese want to say about past or present use of American power in ways affecting China. Such an attitude on our part, such an effort, will take much imagination and much patience. But as Christians we should never give up the effort to reach an understanding with Chinese fellow-Christians and with the Chinese people as persons. We must also continue to urge our governments to persist in efforts to reduce the present strains in relations with the Chinese nation-state.

Footnotes

1. A. M. Halpern (ed.), *Policies Toward China: Views from Six Continents.* New York: McGraw, 1965, p. 104.

2. Robert Blum, *The United States and China in World Affairs.* New York: McGraw, 1967, p. 166. This is the judicious summary volume of the series organized by and published for the Council on Foreign Relations under the same title.

3. A. M. Halpern, *op. cit.*, p. 117.

4. Stanley R. Tupper and D. L. Bailey, *One Continent —Two Voices: The Future of Canada/U.S. Relations.* Toronto: Clarke, Irwin, 1965, pp. 108, 44, 57.

5. *A Conference Report: Canadian-American Relations,* Fourth Annual Orvil A. Dryfoos Conference on Public Affairs. The Public Affairs Center, Dartmouth College, Dartmouth, N. H., 1967, p. 70.

6. *The Interchurch News,* March, 1966.

7. *The Interchurch News,* March, 1968.

8. Central Conference of American Rabbis, *Yearbook,* 1966, p. 52.

9. *Ecumenical Review,* XVIII (1966), p. 264.

10. *Acts and Proceedings,* Ninety-Fourth General Assembly of the Presbyterian Church in Canada, 1968, pp. 206-207.

Summary and Conclusion

M. Searle Bates

CERTAINLY the Chinese nation and its people have demonstrated great capacities in cultural creation, in social and governmental accomplishment through long millennia, in unending labor. Though revolution has now obscured continuity, though poverty still limits life, we can discern in past and present the broad traits described by Professor Boorman—unity, vigor, independence. Add mass, and the outlook is for China to share with Russia and the United States primacy in power and influence. Some global historians would note further that three major streams of civilization stand out preeminent: the Near East and European, now called Western; the Indian; the Chinese.

RECAPITULATION

China paid a heavy price in the nineteenth and early twentieth centuries for isolation from a modernizing and demanding West. In an era when population encroached on food supply, when institutions and rulers were not sufficiently flexible, external pressures insisted upon access to China. New ideas, new goods, new wants outran actual reform, actual production. The old institutions and leadership gave way but were not adequately replaced. Factional and regional rivalries, the competitive rise of the Nationalists and the Communists, the tremendous damage of Japanese encroachment and the overthrow of the Nationalist regime by the Communist, have been surveyed by Professor Wilbur. Meanwhile, during this same tumultuous era, the foundations of future progress were being laid. A transportation network of railways and highways was slowly built and a system of modern postal service and telecommunication was developed; modern banking was provided, with the dangerous advantages of expansive currency; education was considerably developed, as was the nucleus of modern health services; a fair start was made in power manufacturing and mining, led by textiles; new and improved crops made a real difference in many areas. Invaluable resources and personnel were at hand when the Communists finally won control.

The political and military failure of the Nationalists in the face of the Japanese invasion and its aftermath made the discipline, vigor and initial moderation of the Communists look bright. Professor Chen has enabled us to sense the tre-

SUMMARY AND CONCLUSION

mendous organizing effort, effectual but harsh and all-compelling, which destroyed opposition, overpowered the reluctant, marshalled the casual. The complex of means included propaganda, group dynamics, control of food-shelter-jobs, pervasive policing, forced labor, prison and killing when that was deemed economical. For ten years, accomplishment seemed substantial and swift, though the cost in regimentation and hardship was heavy. The forced change in way of life for more than 400,000,000 peasants was a revolution within a revolution, unparalleled in world history for mass and speed, and largely lacking in tangible reward because crops had to be taken from these platooned farmers to supply the vast bureaucracy, army, swelling industries and cities.

Confident planners rushed to the Great Leap Forward of 1958 with commune projects so utopian in ambition as to bring shudders in Moscow. Collapse and retreat were serious checks indeed. The intraparty controversies of that time are now being gradually revealed as they continue in the confused struggles of the Cultural Revolution. The years since the Great Leap seem to have brought food production back to about the level of that earlier time, and they show recovery of industrial advance in some important lines. But who, today, can be sure that a political trend for the vast system has been established? Contention for power and place, as well as for principle and policy, is evident. Yet there is also the claim, impressive to some foreign visitors, that a new ideal, a new type, of common man is being forged by never-faltering indoctrination and the radical shrinking of practical possibilities for sin and selfishness. This claim cannot be scorned. Yet Mao and his cohorts continue to denounce the bourgeois tendencies of the peasants and the capitalist leanings of the President of the People's Republic, who for two decades has been the ethical instructor of party members.

China's foreign relations are not a dull and simple story of disrupt and conquer. Professor Buss does us the important service of letting us see them as from Peking, alongside the experience and response of other countries. Four successive phases of policy within twenty years demonstrate flexibility in tactics, and perhaps in short-range targets. We have also observed the differentials in China's foreign relations according to geographical position, the political character of other states, the economic or political objective holding primacy in China's dealing with one or more states in a certain period. National interest, Communist interest, China's own brand of world revolution, current need for oil, wheat, machinery—all have contended or blended in the mix. No single or simple characterization is truthful. Certainly it is less than wise simply to lump China's role in world affairs as either "belligerency unlimited" or "injured innocence."

SUMMARY AND CONCLUSION

The explicitly Christian factor in the content of this book is found in Christian missions, their character, problems and results in Chinese lives; in the churches and Christian community, resulting from the missionary effort but increasingly Chinese in leadership and expression; in the significance of Chinese Christianity for the churches of North America and the world; and in the present duty of the Christians of the United States and Canada, both as citizens and as believers. Since mission connections were brought to an end twenty years ago, a new generation of North American Christians has developed. It does not have the advantage of the old channels of information, both personal and printed, concerning missions as such, the Chinese Christian community, the society and culture in which the Christian effort was put forth. Neither does it have the deep sense of personal involvement the older generation had known. While some stalwarts of stubbornness or faith have looked forward to resumption of missionary contacts with the main Chinese nation, and some have found continuing good cause in Hong Kong, Taiwan and other East Asian areas, a large part of the Western public, including many North American Christians, has experienced a sense of futility and even of rejection for the whole Christian effort in and on behalf of China. And in the background is an immense volume of hostile criticism, loud over Asia, Africa and elsewhere, in which an intense Nationalist reaction to all that is European-American, "imperialist," "capitalist" and "colonial" is often blended with Communist ideas and slogans. General falterings and perplexities of faith are common among members of American and Canadian churches.

The revolution in China is shock and problem enough. To understand some part of it and to find or maintain a wholesome attitude toward the Chinese people is hard for many of us. We who are Christians need to conserve and to adapt progressively our experience, tradition and concern. Dr. Merwin has truthfully sketched for us the Christian situation in recent China, its strength and weakness, its toil and distress. Ready to accept and to learn from any criticism that has substance, we do not want to lose the reality of this Christian experience in a cloud of slurs arising from moods and ideologies rather than from knowledge. Concern for the Christian community as it was, and for Christians as they now are, is a door to understanding of Chinese citizens in every occupation and locality—the relatives, friends, neighbors of the Christians who themselves share the culture, the economic life, the education and now the all-pervading governmental services and controls of the entire Chinese nation.

In the chapter on the relations of the United States and Canada with China, as well as in the historical chapter by Professor Wilbur and the policy chapter by Professor Buss, we have sensed

SUMMARY AND CONCLUSION

the heavy emotional involvement of the United States; its strong commitment to the National government as over against Japan, thereby lining up reluctantly in the civil war against the Communists; the aggravating factors of Soviet-American competition and of the Korean War; the renewed and confirmed alliance with the Chiang regime as part of a defense system that is actually heavily American, despite wider association. By contrast, the Canadian political stance was more open to perceiving Peking as the unmistakable and presumably enduring center of authority for a renewed, dynamic Chinese nation.

The Christian factor did not have major political significance. But the connections of churches and missions assisted considerable elements in the United States, both Catholic and Protestant, toward sympathetic understanding of those who did not promote the rise of communism. Among these, the group most conspicuous and accessible was the 2,000,000 or more Chinese who fled to Taiwan. By contrast, the long-time Christian contacts of the main Taiwanese population (Chinese who migrated there in earlier generations) were with England and Canada. Recent developments among both Catholics and Protestants include association and adjustment between "mainlanders" and "Taiwanese," but basic differences of historical experience, of language and of ecclesiastical connections have not been readily overcome. Taiwan as such is not our subject. We are here attempting to understand the somewhat separated backgrounds of Canadian (and British) Protestants, while observing the traits of the American connections; and this in the presence of excellent consultative and cooperative relationships between the mission centers of Toronto and New York. (Catholic effort in Taiwan before 1950 was extremely small; it was most sympathetically related to the Nationalist regime at the time of migration, and later, in vigorous enlargement, it has reached out to all elements of the population.)

TOWARD A BETTER FUTURE

1. First and last, we North Americans need to inform ourselves, sympathetically and factually, about the Chinese as persons. We must understand their ways of life, ideas, outlook, whether or not we can substantially approve or "agree with" them. Extraordinary effort is required because of comprehensive revolutionary change.

2. We who are citizens of the United States should realize that American power in Asia is alien power. Our employment of it in China up to 1949, in the North Korean thrust by MacArthur, in alliance with the Nationalist government of Taiwan and in Vietnam has not given the world confidence in our wisdom, steadiness or consideration for the interests and the feelings of other peoples.

SUMMARY AND CONCLUSION

3. In this book's concern for China and her relationships, there is a natural presumption that the conflict in Vietnam would best not end in decisive triumph for the Communist forces, which would encourage further revolutionary adventure and discourage East Asian nations that desire other systems. Nor should it end in decisive defeat for the Communist forces, which might provoke intense resentment and revenge and quite possibly result in much more Chinese direction in all Communist states and parties in Asia, along with temptations for American and other non-Communist factors to rely on force rather than on political and economic improvement. It may well be that costly disappointment for both is preferable (though this is an editorial attitude directed to the China relationships as such, which might have to be modified for reasons of Vietnam proper or of other international concerns). And this attitude is challenged from either side.

4. A good deal of enlightened opinion, illustrated in American and Canadian church statements, advocates recognition of the Peking government and its admission to the United Nations, with continuance of independent status for Taipei. This outlook is supported, explicitly or implicitly, by most of our contributors and the editor. Yet its limitations must be stated. There are no present grounds for hope that either of "the two Chinas," much less *both* of them, would agree. In this situation, it is the part

of statesmanship to foster a climate in which war is not threatened, in the hope that indirect contacts between the two may eventually arise, making an adjustment at a later period less difficult. Neither of the two regimes, nor the international setting, will be the same in 1980 or 1990 as it is today. Gradual changes or a sharp shift within one or both regimes might tend toward some form of association or union. International changes, serious friction between the Taipei government and the United States, active conflict between China and Russia, or acute issues with Japan might alter the problem and the climate. It is to be hoped that the Peking regime will become more flexible and tolerant. It is also to be hoped that Taipei will take more adequate account of the equities and desires of the Taiwanese, on whom the well-being of the island depends. We do not desire to exaggerate the Taiwan issue. But it so often obscures our central concern for relationships with the whole Chinese nation that it must be faced, in the best spirit and mind we can summon.

5. The effort, in the face of isolation, hostility and risk, to avoid extensive war is tremendously urgent. But the beginning and the end are in human attitudes—the slow, manifold overcoming of isolation and hostility, the rich rewards to be found in a humanity of common benefit. Absence of war is a necessary good, but a meager one. As enlightened citizens, as Christians with faith and vision, we look far beyond a snarling

SUMMARY AND CONCLUSION

coexistence of conflicting nations to a kingdom of man, a Kingdom of God, where Chinese, North Americans and all peoples share in productive labor; in health, knowledge and culture; in the life of the spirit. If that is politics, let us accept the accusation. If that is Christian otherworldliness, let us have more of it. Meanwhile, we confront the enemies ignorance, prejudice, self-interest; and the hard realities, the harsh decisions or the reckless drift of every day in Washington and Ottawa, in Peking and Taipei, and in other capitals deeply concerned.

Hostile isolation beholds no future. China, the Chinese people, the issues they raise for us and the world, require far more of mind and heart than we have given.

Recommendations for Further Reading

(Paperbacks—Pa. Out of print—OP: such items are readily available in most libraries.)

A. The Persistent Culture of a Remarkable People

1. Reischauer, Edwin O. and John K. Fairbank, *A History of East Asian Civilization*. Boston: Houghton, 1960, 1965 (2 vols.). Respected for overall competence.

2. Goodrich, L. Carrington, *Short History of the Chinese People*. New York: Harper, 1959 (3rd. rev. ed.). Pa. Packed with specifics of culture.

3. Loewe, Michael, *Imperial China*. New York: Praeger, 1966. Topical treatment of society and institutions.

4. Dawson, Raymond (ed.), *The Legacy of China*. New York: Oxford, 1964. Aspects of culture.

5. DeBary, W. Theodore (ed.), *Sources of Chinese Tradition*. New York: Columbia, 1960 (2 vols.). Pa. Superb choice and presentation of ideas from antiquity to Mao.

B. The Modernizing Revolutions: Nationalist and Communist

1. Fairbank, John K., *The United States and China*. New York: Viking, 1962 (rev. ed.). Pa. Mostly China; perhaps the best single introduction.

2. Fitzgerald, C. P., *The Birth of Communist China*. Baltimore: Penguin, 1964. Pa. Perspective on how and why it came to be.

3. Cressey, George B., *Land of the 500 Million: A Geography of China*. New York: McGraw, 1955. Nature, resources, man.

4. Clubb, O. Edmund, *Twentieth Century China*. New York: Columbia, 1963. Pa. Political and military emphases.

5. Schram, Stuart R., *Mao Tse-Tung*. New York: Simon and Schuster, 1967. Excellent scholarship, covering work and thought.

6. *Mao Tse-Tung, Political Thought of*, tr. and ed. by Stuart R. Schram. New York: Praeger, 1963. Pa. The best selections and introduction for serious study.

7. *Mao Tse-Tung, Quotations from Chairman* (with introduction by A. Doak Barnett). New York: Bantam, 1967. Pa. The "red book" of tossed slogans; needs a guide.

8. MacInnis, Donald E., "Maoism: The Religious Analogy," see D-12.

9. Snow, Edgar, *Red Star Over China*. New York: Grove, 1961. Pa. (Rev. ed., hard cover, 1968.) This classic of reporting is now extended by the author's recent visits and reading.

10. Chicago China Conference, *Contemporary China* (Ruth Adams, ed.). New York: Random, 1966. Selections from fifteen diverse authors.

11. Chen, Theodore H. E., *The Communist Regime: Documents and Commentary.* New York: Praeger, 1968. Pa. An excellent and considerable collection.

12. Boorman, Howard L., "The Social Revolution in Contemporary China," see D-12.

13. Barnett, A. Doak, *China after Mao: with Selected Documents.* Princeton: Princeton University Press, 1967. Pa. Thoughtful search for trends.

14. Taylor, Charles, *Reporter in Red China.* New York: Random, 1966. A good instance of Canadian observation.

C. International Relations and Attitudes

1. Blum, Robert and A. Doak Barnett, *The United States and China in World Affairs.* New York: McGraw, 1966. Pa. This sound and generalizing volume, like the two following, is in the series undertaken by the Council on Foreign Relations under the same title.

2. Halpern, A. M. (ed.), *Policies Toward China: Views from Six Continents.* New York: McGraw, 1965. Pa. Excellent essays from 16 countries or regions, seeing also China's policies toward them.

3. Steele, Archibald T., *The American People and China.* New York: McGraw, 1966. Pa. Concerned with information/ignorance, and with attitudes.

4. Hinton, Harold C., *Communist China in World Politics.* Boston: Houghton, 1966. Carefully organized specific information and judgments.

5. Hinton, Harold C., "China and Vietnam"; James C. Hsiung, "China's Foreign Policy"; Dick Wilson, "China in East and South Asia"; John M. H. Lindbeck, "China and the World"; see D-12.

6. Bennett, John C., "Christian Perspective on

the Communist Revolution"; William W. Lockwood, "China and the Peace of Asia"; see D-11.

7. Tupper, Stanley R. and Douglas L. Bailey, *Canada and the United States: The Second Hundred Years*. New York: Hawthorn, 1967. Title in Canada: *One Continent—Two Voices: The Future of Canada /U.S. Relations*. Toronto: Clarke, Irwin, 1967.

D. The Christian Factor

1. Latourette, Kenneth S., *A History of Christian Missions in China*. 1929 (reprinted by Paragon and by Russell). Substantial classic, to be supplemented by following items.

2. Ballou, Earle H., *Dangerous Opportunity: The Christian Mission in China Today*. New York: Friendship, 1940. OP.

3. Price, Frank W., *China: Twilight or Dawn?* New York: Friendship, 1948. OP.

4. Jones, Francis P., *The Church in Communist China*. New York: Friendship, 1962. Pa.

5. Jones, Francis P. (ed.), *Documents of the Three-Self Movement: Materials for the Study of the Protestant Church in Communist China*. Asia Department: NCC, 1963. Pa.

6. Bates, M. Searle: "The Church in China in the Twentieth Century," see D-11; "Christianity in the People's Republic of China," see D-12; "The Fate of Christianity in China," *Christianity and Crisis*, May 13, 1968; "Christianity in the People's Republic: A Time for Study to Understand," in *China Notes*, Asia Department, National Council of Churches, April, 1968.

7. Stowe, David M., "Christian Responsibility Now toward Witness in China," see D-11.

8. Merwin, Wallace C., "Chinese Christians and the Ecumenical Community"; William J. Richardson, "Sino-Vatican Relations Since 1949"; see D-11.

9. Varg, Paul A., *Missionaries, Chinese, and Diplomats: The American Protestant Missionary Movement in China, 1890-1952*. Princeton: Princeton University Press, 1958. Stimulating studies by a political scientist.

10. Paton, David M., *Christian Mission and the Judgment of God*. London: SCM, 1953; and Naperville: Allenson. OP. Somewhat personal but influential critique of China missions from within.

11. Richardson, William J. (ed.), *China and Christian Responsibility*. New York: Maryknoll/Friendship, 1968. Pa. This and the following present materials from conferences under Protestant auspices, much of it listed in preceding sections by author and topic.

12. Richardson, William J. (ed.), *China Today*. New York: Maryknoll/Friendship, 1968. Pa. Somewhat centered on international relations. A group of documents is included.

13. MacInnis, Donald E. (ed.), *China Notes*, quarterly. Asia Department, Division of Overseas Ministries, NCC, Room 612, 475 Riverside Drive, New York, N. Y. 10027. A concise report of trends and ideas in contemporary China, undertaken with Christian concern.

About the Contributors

M. SEARLE BATES

Searle Bates is a graduate of Hiram College, who took bachelor's and master's degrees at Oxford University in history and a doctorate at Yale University, with a further year at Harvard. From 1920 to 1950 he represented the United Christian Missionary Society (Disciples of Christ) at the University of Nanking as Professor of History. He was a member of the China Council on Christian Higher Education, 1924-1950. Dr. Bates served the National Christian Council of China in various capacities from 1937, and the International Missionary Council from 1938 to 1959. He was Professor of Missions at Union Theological Seminary, New York, 1950-1965. He has worked in various departments and commissions of the National Council of Churches, U.S.A., and the World Council of Churches, in capacities concerned with China, international affairs and religious liberty, and has written on these subjects for various publications. His chief book was *Religious Liberty: an*

Inquiry, published in several languages but suppressed in China. He is now studying and writing toward a large work on Christianity in Chinese society and culture since 1900.

HOWARD L. BOORMAN

Howard Boorman is Professor of History at Vanderbilt University. A graduate of the University of Wisconsin, he did nearly four years of intensive study of the Chinese and Japanese languages at the University of Colorado, Yale and Peiping. Foreign Service Officer at Peiping (Peking), 1947-1950, and Hong Kong, 1950-1954, he organized and developed the comprehensive press monitoring and translation service that has been a major source of information originating in China. Since then his main work has been the creation and construction of the four-volume collaborative *Biographical Dictionary of Republican China,* 1967-1969, a collection of biographies of several hundred Chinese prominent in public life, which is almost a history of China in this century. Professor Boorman has contributed frequently to professional journals and symposia.

C. MARTIN WILBUR

Martin Wilbur spent his boyhood in China, where his father was a YMCA secretary in Shanghai. An Oberlin graduate, he did his doctoral work at Columbia University and then served for seven years as Curator of Chinese Ethnology and Archeology at the Field Museum, Chicago. Since 1947, Dr. Wilbur has been Professor of Chinese History at Columbia University and, for several years, concurrently Director of the East Asian Institute. He has published

ABOUT THE CONTRIBUTORS

Slavery in China During the Former Han Dynasty and, with Julie How, *Documents on Communism, Nationalism and Soviet Advisers in China, 1918-1927*. In recent years, Professor Wilbur has given major attention to the century from 1850 to 1950 in Chinese history. He is currently engaged in extensive writing on the Republican-Nationalist period.

THEODORE HSI-EN CHEN

Theodore H. E. Chen was born in Foochow and took his A.B. at Fukien Christian University. He received his master's degree from Columbia University and his doctor's from the University of Southern California. Dr. Chen served his Chinese alma mater as Professor of Education and Dean, 1929-1937, and later as Acting President, 1946-1947. Since 1938 he has been at the University of Southern California as Professor of Education and of Asian Studies; and since 1941 has also been head of the Department of Asiatic Studies and Director of the East Asian Studies Center. Author of many articles and monographs on contemporary China, Professor Chen has published two major books: *Thought Reform of the Chinese Intellectuals*, 1960; and *The Chinese Communist Regime, Documents and Commentary*, 1967.

CLAUDE A. BUSS

Claude Buss did graduate work at Susquehanna University and his doctorate at the University of Pennsylvania. He then served in China as a member of the United States Foreign Service, 1927-1934. Dr. Buss was Professor of International Relations at the University of Southern California, 1934-1941, and since 1946 has been at Stanford as Professor of History. He has edited, with extensive introductions, two small books of documents: *The People's Republic of China*, 1962; and *Southeast Asia and the World Today*, 1958. His larger books represent the wider interests shown in his essay for this symposium: *War and Diplomacy in Eastern Asia*, 1941; *Arc of Crisis*, 1961; and *Asia in the Modern World*, 1964 (East and Southeast Asia).

WALLACE C. MERWIN

Wallace Merwin is a graduate of the University of Louisville and of the Louisville Presbyterian Theological Seminary, and holds a master's degree in theology from Union Seminary, New York. From 1931 to 1950, he served the North China Mission of the Presbyterian Church USA, basically at Paoting, but from 1945 in Peiping and Shanghai with executive responsibilities. He had broad experience in student work, teaching and war relief, and served as secretary of the (Presbyterian) China Council and of the National Christian Council. Since 1953, he has been Secretary of the Far Eastern Office, the China Committee and latterly the Asia Department of the National Council of Churches, U.S.A., traveling and consulting frequently in Hong Kong, Taiwan and other areas of the Far East.

E. BRUCE COPLAND

Bruce Copland was born in Montreal, graduated from McGill University in 1922 and began immediate service in Honan (North Central China) with the Canadian Presbyterian Mission (soon to enter the United Church of Canada, in which he has worked since). He did advanced theological study,

ABOUT THE CONTRIBUTORS

1926-1929, in Montreal, Edinburgh and Paris, and then was in Taiwan, 1929-1931, before returning to China for service in Honan, Szechuan and Shanghai until 1951. In the last ten years of that stormy period, Mr. Copland was Executive Secretary of the Church of Christ in China. From 1952 to 1957 he served the National Council of Churches, U.S.A., as secretary for missionary personnel. He returned to Taiwan in 1957 and from 1959 till his retirement in 1965 was Associate General Secretary of the Presbyterian Church of Formosa.

CHINA IN CHANGE

an approach to understanding

edited by M. Searle Bates

FRIENDSHIP PRESS   NEW YORK

Library of Congress Catalog
Card Number: 68-57710

Copyright © 1969 by Friendship Press, Inc.
Printed in the United States of America

Preface

THE CHINESE, the most numerous people of mankind, are largely isolated from the international community, are formally at war with the United Nations and live in mutual hostility with many other peoples. How can this be? For the well-being and peace of the entire world, it is important that the situation be understood and dealt with.

We of the United States and Canada are responsible for exercising enlightened citizenship, and for working to affect the policies of our governments so that we can reach out into manifold relationships with other peoples, including the Chinese. In this task Christians participate with others, recognizing that the general human duty rests upon us with even a greater responsibility because of the commitments of our faith, our missionary experience and our ecumenical acquaintance and brotherhood.

Is this book politics and history, a secular study of power and conflict with some human elements of social and cultural interest? Is it a book on foreign missions, perhaps broadened by comments on revolution, communism and war? Neither, and both. Competent and respected professors from the history departments and research enterprises concerned with China at Columbia, Vanderbilt, Southern California and Stanford Universities portray the position of that country in the life of the world, paying special attention to recent and current changes within China and in its relationships. An American and a Canadian churchman, each with long experience and exceptional knowledge of the Christian enterprises among the Chinese, make their appropriate contributions.

This symposium stands in a great tradition of interdenominational mission study books, which over a span of seventy years have informed church members about the Chinese people—their distinctive humanity, their culture, their needs and problems and the nurturing of a Chinese Christian community through sharing in work and service. Now direct missionary connection with the church in China has been decisively broken, and the Chinese churches have experienced extraordinary changes and difficulties. The Chinese people have entered upon a massive revolution unique in all history, startling and perplexing to most North Americans, and carrying with it aspects of isolation and conflict that bring anxiety to the thoughtful. We believe, therefore, that the relevant Christian mission at this moment is to seek, with the best available resources, *understanding* of the Chinese people and of what we can do as Christians to improve present relationships.

We have neither the arrogance nor the space to try to discuss all the aspects of this vast problem. Some will feel that we attempt too much; others may complain that we neglect factors important to them, such as the challenge of Communist ideology to Christian thought, Christian activity in Hong Kong and Taiwan, or a theology of revolution. We have decided, in the interests of convenience and clarity, to direct ourselves to the main body of the Chinese people, of whom 95 percent live in the People's Republic of China, with Peking as capital. For them, we employ the term "China." We are keenly conscious of the will of the regime on Taiwan, with Taipei as capital, to use that name and to lay claim to represent the political and cultural tradition linked with it, under the name Republic of China. These two official names are awkward and confusing to many. Moreover, to call an island, even an important one, "China" is a greater distortion of reality than to use the simple indicator of geography and history, Taiwan (Formosa). Fortunately it was possible to secure for discussion of this question Mr. Bruce Copland, a Canadian with long experience in Central China and later in Taiwan, who has the additional qualification of understanding in his own life the displacement from China to Taiwan and the issues of adjustment in that island between newcomers and the older residents. Our study, then, is centered on the main country and body of people most readily identified in the rest of the world as China and the Chinese, even though millions of persons of Chinese race, in varying cultural and political status, are to be found in Taiwan, Hong Kong, Singapore and elsewhere.

The Department of Education for Mission of the National Council of Churches set for its adult program on China several objectives: To help North American Christians (1) to understand the contemporary history, culture and influence of the Chinese people; (2) to appreciate the Chinese people as fellow members of the family of nations and as persons made in the image of God, making a great contribution to humanity; (3) to find ways to influence public opinion on the positions and relations of their governments to China. Guidelines coming from the denominational representatives provided for a symposium that would include diverse contributions, and even "controversy." The writers understood this last term as (1) readiness to face difficult issues, on which differing judgments are recognized and expected; and (2) readiness to challenge, according to the contributors' knowledge and sense of truth, attitudes and opinions common in parts of our citizenry and church.

PREFACE

Attitudes frequently found in North America include: (1) Indifference and lack of information; prejudice and distortion linked to slight or outdated knowledge. (2) Shock and perplexity over the Communist conquest of China and its consequences in (a) novel political and economic operations; (b) military effectiveness in Korea and in nuclear potential; (c) the decisive break in Christian missions, followed by forced attrition of the churches and now by the extinguishing of visible religion; (d) repeated proclamation of world revolution as goal or program. (3) Stereotypes of China as completely wrong; incessantly aggressive; a mechanism and not a nation of human beings; an unchanging force under one demonic will; or a new heaven from which poverty and selfishness are gone, a nation progressing remarkably, under communism, from an entire and evil darkness before 1949. (4) Additional perplexity over the claim of the Taiwan regime, with which the United States is allied and which has recently made significant economic improvement, to be the true Republic of China and the bearer of Chinese civilization. We in North America often use the term "Two Chinas." Sharply repudiated both in Peking and in Taipei, this view demands of an intelligent advocate that he should not loosely equate or confuse the two present entities, but should always be conscious of the extent and character of each.

Each of the six authors of this symposium carries responsibility for what he has written, the editor for the Preface and Conclusion. No line has been pressed upon any one; integrity of thought and statement, even to the point of mutual contradiction, has from the first been assured. We ask of our readers only that they discuss any statement made here with due regard for its total context.

M. SEARLE BATES

Contents

Preface
  M. Searle Bates   5

Chapter 1
  China: Yesterday and Tomorrow
  Howard L. Boorman   13

Chapter 2
  China's Transitional Century, 1850-1950
  C. Martin Wilbur   33

Chapter 3
  People's Republic of China, 1949-1968
  Theodore H. E. Chen   63

Chapter 4
  China and the Chinese Among the Nations
  Claude A. Buss   89

Chapter 5
 Christianity in the Life of
 the Chinese People
  Wallace C. Merwin   116

Chapter 6
 China, Canada and the United States:
 A Canadian Perspective
  E. Bruce Copland   143

Summary and Conclusion
 M. Searle Bates   171

Recommendations for Further Reading   182

About the Contributors   187

China: Yesterday and Tomorrow

Howard L. Boorman

CHINA, like classical Greece, has shown herself in many guises to many observers, depending on their temperament, training and intuition.

CHINA AND THE WORLD POWER TRIANGLE

To the intelligent foreigner, the most prominent fact in China is the poverty of its people. There are too many villages to the square mile, too many families to the village, too many "mouths" to the family. Wherever one goes, it is the same weary tale with interminable reiteration. Poverty, poverty, poverty, always and evermore poverty.[1]

With these words, written seventy years ago, Dr. Arthur Smith, the famous missionary and student of China, identified grinding poverty as the most conspicuous element in the Chinese social and physical landscape. Today that poverty is perhaps the least emphasized fact amid the millions of words used by Western observers to analyze the turmoil of China today and to predict the course of China tomorrow. Old China hands stress the essential, though elusive, element of Chineseness in Mao Tse-tung's New China. Strategic theorists debate the implications of Peking's growing nuclear capabilities. Policy planners in Washington take some comfort in the upheaval of the Cultural Revolution, which lends a tinge of rationality to the policies of those governments diplomatically allied with Chiang Kai-shek in Taiwan. Countless discussion groups assess the ambiguities of American Far Eastern policy, circulate petitions demanding a new look at Asia beyond Vietnam and find themselves unwitting followers of the well-known adage of Sun Yat-sen: *Hsing-i, chih-nan* ("To act is easy, to understand is difficult"). Mao Tse-tung's "Red Book" has been a solid seller throughout the West.

The responsible citizen, already harassed by inflation, rising taxes, generational conflict, violence in the inner city and population pressures, is hardly to be blamed if he leaves serious appraisal of the China problem to the China experts. But the experts often disagree among themselves. While the Secretary of State reiterates his concern at the long-range threat to American interests in Asia posed by Communist China, many remain unimpressed with the coherence, relevance or even common sense of United States China policy in 1969. The urgent national need remains to create a meaningful framework within which to view the China of the future.

The three powers likely to play a dominant role in world affairs from 1970 to 2000 are the United States, the Union of Soviet Socialist Republics and the People's Republic of China. Two of these nations are already super-powers with global interests and commitments. Communist China's future is more debatable, for her capabilities are more limited and her interests more clearly related to East Asia than to the arena of global power. But the leaders at Peking are clearly aware of the distinctive position of China as the first major area of the non-Western world to launch a complete social revolution aimed at modernization and industrialization. And even less-committed observers estimate that the linguistic environment of the future is likely to be dominated by English, Russian and Chinese.

Interestingly, the United States, the Soviet Union and the People's Republic of China share several attributes as great continental powers. Each possesses the necessary population and raw materials for sustained industrial development. Each, at least in its present incarnation, is a relatively young nation in the modern world. Each manifests that blend of oversensitivity and overconfidence characteristic of land-based nations that have lived largely to themselves. Each is inclined to depend more on conventional territorial spheres of influence than on international organization to achieve its major political objectives. Each, at the same time, is totally convinced of the validity and inner logic of its own political-economic-social system and is deadly serious about exporting to the rest of the world the doctrines supporting that system. Each, finally, is fearful that the other two mastodons will soon join (if they have not already secretly joined) in an unholy, long-range alliance to block its rightful aspirations.

Professional analysis of the American-Russian-Chinese power triangle and of the variables affecting its conflicting interests is frequently so subtle and overcomplicated that it is of scant use to the layman. Oversimplification may therefore be a necessary prelude to understanding. Our concern in this chapter is essentially with historical perspective. We will look, first, at Western, particularly North American, thinking about China as an element affecting our long-term relations with East Asia. Then we will look at selected aspects of the Chinese past that are likely to affect the pattern of China tomorrow.

Some United States Perspectives on China

Many American assumptions regarding the China problem since 1950 have been influenced by the attitudes and aspirations that shaped the American view of China before the Communist conquest of power on the mainland and the removal of the government of the Republic of China to Taiwan.

For reasons perhaps more domestic than external, what may be labeled American romanticism toward China and the Chinese people became, over the course of a century, ingrained both in American thinking and, to an extent, in American diplomacy. One key element was the early clipper ship trade that linked Puritan Salem and imperial Canton in incongruous tandem. In the late eighteenth century, shortly after the American Revolution and after the period of the vigorous early emperors of the Ch'ing Dynasty in China, the search for new horizons, new markets and new adventures led American sailing ships around the Horn and the Cape of Good Hope to penetrate the Pearl River in South China. Frustration engendered by the conflict between Chinese obstinacy and "squeeze" on the one hand, and Yankee shrewdness on the other, did not obscure the lucrative nature of the commerce. Some at least of America's first great family fortunes emerged from the China trade.

These early contacts had both economic and cultural consequences. Throughout the nineteenth century, trading interest in China was nurtured by statistics and fed by the potential consumer demand of China's millions. At another level, the attraction of China was aesthetic. Born in a raw environment, raised in the stern simplicity of life on a developing frontier, Americans were deeply affected by the discovery across the Pacific of a settled, proud and urbane land, steeped in the subtlety of a civilization so ancient that nothing except the West was new. Drawn with a sense of romantic attachment to the cultural unity of China and with an antiquarian admiration for the achievements of its Mandarin élite, republican America came to seek the preservation of traditional China's relics.

Still another key factor in the development of early American attitudes toward the Central Kingdom was the missionary impulse. Initially this zeal was evangelistic, an aspect of the upsurge of Protestant missionary enterprise that affected many parts of the world during the last century. Gradually, however, the proselytizing spirit of evangelism led to direct missionary involvement with and discreet missionary pressure upon United States governmental policies toward China. During the first half of the twentieth century in particular, the missionary impulse came to affect the style of American policy. The United States assumed a self-imposed moral responsibility for shielding China and the Chinese from the depredations of "imperialist" nations (European, then Japanese); and doing good in China came to be a minor hallmark on our national coat of arms. Through the broadening impulse associated with the missionary enterprise, the United States developed a vicarious emotional involvement in the affairs of China that far exceeded the extent of our practical interests there.

CHINA: YESTERDAY AND TOMORROW

Both trading interests and missionary impulses contributed historically to shaping American attitudes toward China. The missionary, however, played a far more active role than did the businessman in molding American opinion, and many Americans who never saw China or knew a Chinese had their images created by missionary reports. The individual Protestant American saw China largely as a challenge for Christianization; while Americans, in their corporate role as a fortunate and friendly people, found relief from a sense of guilt for United States affluence by patterning the Chinese in our likeness: potential Americans to be modernized, sanitized and converted. With altruism not unmarred by condescension, we gave generously to a starving China, never seriously doubting that the Chinese whom we sought to save were basically as democratic, as steadfastly righteous and as fundamentally individualistic as we conceived ourselves to be.

Seen in retrospect, American commitment to the fallacies underlying American mythology about China and the Chinese was both devoted and disastrous. It is small wonder that other nations of the world found the American image of China largely unintelligible and substantially inconsistent with the models they, from their own national psychologies and national interests, had fashioned. And it is hardly surprising that American policies constructed on these fallacies floundered during the 1940's when the

United States confronted in China a revolutionary war waged by the Communists against the Nationalists.

By then the clock had gone full circle. Ever since the Open Door notes of 1899-1900, American policy had aimed at the preservation of the administrative and territorial integrity of China. Suddenly, ironically, almost without warning because it had either ignored or misread the storm signals, the United States found itself faced with that relatively strong and relatively unified China of which it had long dreamed. Since 1950, the dilemma of United States policy has been the development of patterns of understanding and behavior necessary to coexist and to share the same ocean with a Communist China both able and determined to preserve its territorial and administrative integrity, and its political autonomy, without direct assistance from the United States or any other nation.

Chinese Civilization: Past Carries into Present

The China of tomorrow will be both Chinese and Communist according to its own definitions. Even with the disruption of the Cultural Revolution since 1966, Chinese attitudes in the long run will still be affected significantly by past patterns of Chinese history. It is thus essential to attempt to place today's headlines in perspective, to take a longer look at China as the only major area of the world that developed down to recent times totally outside Western control or domination and to assess the ways in which China's tomorrow may be shaped by her long series of yesterdays.[2]

Western interest in China has consistently run ahead of Western capacity to understand it, for the social and linguistic barriers to comprehension have been and remain formidable. The society of China is one of relatively few that independently developed the size and complexity, the technical mastery over environment and the artistic and intellectual creativity that mark a major civilization. Early man developed in the Yellow River Valley of North China in circumstances comparable to those that stimulated the early riverine civilizations of Egypt and Mesopotamia. The Shang and early Chou periods in China were roughly contemporaneous with the empires of the ancient Near East: the Egyptian, Babylonian, Assyrian and Persian.

Classical China of the late Chou and Han eras was a contemporary of the classical civilizations of the Western world. The parallel between the great figures of Greek and Chinese philosophy (Plato and Confucius, for example) is striking; the social milieu that stimulated the rise of the philosophical schools was not dissimilar; and the great ages in both Greece and China produced seminal systems that have exercised deep influence on the cultural and intellectual life of East Asia and Western Europe. The traditional view that non-Hellenes were barbarians is even strikingly similar to the classical Chinese view of their relations with non-Chinese peoples.

Chinese philosophical concepts, at once parochial and universal, were sustained in East Asia by cultural superiority and by military dominance. Traditional Chinese culturalism posed a Sinocentric world, unified by the pervasive influence of Sinic civilization and sustained by the august virtue emanating from the Chinese Emperor, the Son of Heaven. This Sinic world extended throughout the Central Kingdom, to adjacent tributary states on the empire's periphery and even to barbarians totally beyond the pale. In the political-military sphere, the two most enduring empires of recorded history were those of Rome and China. While the power of Rome waned and collapsed in the fifth century, the Chinese imperial system lasted from Han times to the early twentieth century.

Viewed as a whole, Chinese history is the record of the gradual expansion of the agrarian Chinese people over a continental-size area in the face of difficult obstacles created both by the forces of nature and by recurrent invasions of nomadic peoples from the steppe-lands of Inner Asia. Over the centuries, Chinese civilization became rooted in bureaucratic government and articulated through a hierarchic social structure based on the ethical precepts of Confucius. Confucianism was not a formal religion, but it embodied a table of "thou-shalt's" and "thou-shalt-not's" that determined the norms of social and individual conduct in traditional China. The literate élite of the empire lived, at least nominally, according to the ground rules governing status and obligation set down in the Confucian texts. The illiterate peasant population was deeply affected, even though it was unable to read the Confucian classics.

Perhaps the most impressive aspect of the traditional Chinese system of government was the way that system was administered by a tiny group of men. Because the central goal in traditional Chinese society was academic-bureaucratic success, the governing bureaucracy under the Emperor was indeed the national élite. The main channel for entry into the ruling élite, and a major key to the political and social stability of the Chinese empire, was the competitive examination system established in T'ang times (A.D. 618-907) and lasting until the turn of the present century. Within the limits of traditional Chinese life and thought, the examination system was by far the most impartial and efficient method of identifying men of merit and of recruiting them into the public service. Only the English—and that in recent times—have been as addicted as the Chinese to competitive examinations as a method of guiding and stabilizing a society and an empire.

As the tradition-bound scholar-officials of China wrote Chinese history, they tended to project a self-serving self-image, that of the Central Kingdom as a great humanistic culture, overwhelmingly literary in focus and civilian in instinct. Most Western scholars who studied traditional Chinese civilization not unnaturally tended to reproduce the same image and to regard China as the epitome of sage government.

In reality, the image created by both Chinese and Western scholars must be altered to include at least two other dimensions of traditional Chinese civilization: the military and the scientific. The Chinese military tradition, though compromised by the low social status accorded military officers, was nevertheless venerable and distinguished. All major Chinese dynasties were founded by vigorous individuals capable of organizing and directing military power to attain desired ends. And the empire, notably in the early periods of major dynasties, was not a civil bureaucracy alone. The system also embraced a military apparatus that supported Chinese conquest and expansion into areas on China's geographical periphery, notably in Korea, Mongolia and Turkestan, Tibet, Annam and other areas now labeled Southeast Asia.

Similarly, the scientific dimension of traditional Chinese civilization must be set in perspective. Indeed, the major researches of Dr. Joseph Needham of the University of Cambridge indicate that, from ancient times until about 1400, the Chinese led the world technologically. While the Greeks and Arabs gave much to Western science, the Chinese, Needham repeatedly reminds us, also made major contributions to human scientific development.[3] In the development of modern mechanics, dynamics and celestial and terrestrial physics, the Chinese, at decisive breakthrough points, provided basic knowledge of magnetic phenomena. It is a notable aspect of the contemporary revolution in China since 1950 that the Communists have in fact devoted major attention to the task of refurbishing and buttressing China's military and scientific heritage.

If these dimensions of traditional Chinese civilization remain somewhat murky, because they are insufficiently studied, the literary and artistic dimensions of that civilization were and are recognized to be of world significance. Because of the central position held by the written language in the culture, the ink-charged brush is a key symbol of China; and literature, calligraphy and painting have for centuries been intertwined in the life of China's literate élite. Chinese painting not only enjoyed enormous prestige within China; it also exercised major influence on the art of painting in Japan. Chinese bronzes embodied unusual strength and stylistic form at a very early period. Chinese sculpture and architecture hold major positions in the history of Far Eastern art; Chinese ceramics were similarly celebrated and are today amply illustrated in the principal museums and private collections of Asia, Europe and North America. In the realm where art and craftsmanship blend, Chinese manual and inventive ingenuity has long been famous. Chinese household furniture of the Ming period, for example, combined simplicity, balance and a sense of proportion that equaled, or perhaps excelled, any in the contemporary world. Indeed, Chinese talent in the crafts—lacquer, jade and other precious gems, textiles, wood and other media—is superb. It has been said that virtually every Chinese, from village carpenter to erudite scholar, was in some sense a craftsman.

THE CHINESE PEOPLE: WHAT ARE THEY LIKE?

Generalizations about traditional Chinese civilization should be made with caution; generalizations about the Chinese people must be made with circumspection. Historically, China has been an extraordinarily complex civilization with a wide variety of subcultures. Yet a dominant feature of the Chinese political tradition has been the internal conviction that "China" constitutes a single entity. Cultural patterns, the common written language, classical texts, the fact that more than 90 percent of the population is ethnically Han Chinese, the historical role of China as the major power center and cultural mother of East Asia—and pride in all these factors—have combined to buttress the belief of the Chinese people that they constitute a cohesive group distinct from outsiders.

Among themselves, however, the Chinese are acutely aware of local differences and patterns of regionalism that have long persisted. Differences in spoken language, local customs and traditions and cuisine, even as in physical characteristics and personality traits, were marked over a vast, diverse terrain. Even the casual outsider could see the contrast between the steady, camel-like Northerner and the darting, fish-like Southerner, impetuous and loquacious. The distinctions were actually finer and more subtle, and a substantial folklore developed in China around the differences between the various provinces and their inhabitants. The culturally advanced and equable province of Kiangsu, for example, evoked images of the arts of good living. The people of Kiangsi were the Scots of China: clannish, overfrugal, quarrelsome. The son of Shantung was sturdy, reliable and diligent, but unlikely to capture first place in the imperial examinations. The Hunanese were stubborn, tough soldiers and passionate lovers. Fukien faced the sea, and its separate river valleys were subregions of a physical and cultural province that in a sense turned its back on China to become the most sea-conscious section of the country.

Traditional China was both many and one, and the interaction of historical and geographical factors produced a society as notable for human diversity as for cultural cohesion. Perhaps because of this diversity, Western views of Chinese social and individual behavior have careened among several contradictory images: that the Chinese are basically like the Westerners, with perhaps even some points of superiority, notably in the peasant virtues of simplicity, diligence and cheerfulness; that the Chinese are cowardly, avaricious and callous degenerates; that the Chinese are refined and cultivated sages; that the Chinese are perverse, diabolical fiends; and so on through a bewildering spectrum.

Viewed objectively as a people, the Chinese are clearly neither virtuous nor wicked, neither intelligent nor stupid. At the same time, many patterns of action in China have been and are governed by modes of thought different from those conventionally called "Western." Some "Chinese characteristics" have doubtless been bred by the requirements for existence in a crowded land. The solidarity of the traditional Chinese family system, the subordination of the individual to the collective group, the rules of mutual adaptation and group responsibility: these and other patterns owed as much to the struggle for survival in a predominantly peasant society as they did to the precepts of Confucius.

Paradoxically, the survival formula of the Chinese people is not dissimilar to that enunciated by a character in Dostoevsky for becoming a Rothschild: "It is an infinitely simple matter; the secret consists in two words: obstinacy and continuity."

The obstinate ability of the Chinese to live and to survive under physical and psychological conditions that would quickly defeat the Westerner has long been noted by sensitive observers in China. Dr. Arthur Smith, writing from his long experience in North China, credited the Chinese people with a notable range of characteristics that aided survival: physical vitality, endurance, psychological stamina, absence of nerves, indifference to comfort and convenience and others.[4] Whatever the merits of Dr. Smith's insights, the Chinese as a people have indubitably demonstrated unusual climatic adaptability. From northern Manchuria to the Equator, they have been able to live, to work, to reproduce, to compete and occasionally to prosper. No other people has yet matched the Chinese record in this elemental sphere.

Obstinacy embodies determination. Continuity implies patience, perseverance and a developed sense—or perhaps a developed disregard—of time. The Chinese conception of time is also a distinctive aspect of the Chinese personality. From ancient epochs to the era of Chairman Mao, the Chinese have shown the psychological ability to maintain an objective over unusually long periods of time without succumbing to the impatience or frustration that normally accompanies extended delays. The Chinese is apparently willing to persevere because he knows that persistence will pay off and that an unremitting approach to a goal assures its ultimate attainment.

Writing after World War I, Bertrand Russell

remarked that the Chinese, from the highest to the lowest, "have an imperturbable quiet dignity, which is usually not even destroyed by a European education." Communist actions in the 1950's and 1960's may be producing radical, perhaps profound, discontinuities in Chinese behavior. Yet some traits of the Chinese as people are virtually certain to survive, notably their sense of dignity and their profound pride in being black-haired Chinese. Perhaps the major challenge confronting Western citizens and Western governments today, therefore, is the task of viewing China in its Chinese, no less than in its world, context.

Yet a major obstacle in responding to this challenge is the fact that the West has no baseline from which to measure social change in twentieth century China. The vista of the period from the 1840's to the 1940's is inadequate, if only because China in its late imperial and early republican incarnations was hardly China in a classical period of vitality and confidence. Indeed it is precisely in the psychological sector that the Communists—whatever the outcome of the Cultural Revolution—may have scored their most significant success. Through shrewd linkage of selected aspects of the Chinese tradition and the imperatives of revolutionary modernization, the new rulers in the ancient northern capital have restored self-respect to China as a distinctive cultural entity and as the first modernizing new nation of the non-Western world to gain autonomous access to the levers of thermonuclear power.

Grinding poverty remains today the most omnipresent reality in China. Because of this fact, no matter what Chinese economic growth statistics may reveal or conceal, Chinese society taken as a whole is still struggling with problems of massive backwardness, both human and material, that will take decades to overcome. China can presently attain at best a sort of demi-modernity, in which national power is successfully mobilized in selected sectors, but in which the constant pressure of population on food production seriously inhibits progress on a per capita basis.

For China, to be sure, even demi-modernity on a substantial scale represents progress. And when historians of the future survey the second half of our century, they will surely record the emergence of a relatively unified China from a century of domestic distress and international humiliation as one of the major features of the human story. If any people in the world deserves surcease from the pressures and problems of backwardness, it is the *lao-pai-hsing,* "Old Hundred Names," the obstinate, durable and dignified sons of the Chinese soil.

Footnotes

1. Arthur H. Smith, *Village Life in China.* New York: Revell, 1899, pp. 310 ff.

2. C. P. Fitzgerald, *The Chinese View of Their*

Place in the World. London, New York: Oxford University Press, 1964.

3. Needham's voluminous studies, learned but perhaps overlaudatory, are conveniently presented in his essay, "Science and China's Influence in the World," in Raymond Dawson (ed.), *The Legacy of China*. Oxford, England: Clarendon Press and New York: Oxford University Press, 1964, pp. 234-308.

4. Arthur H. Smith, *Chinese Characteristics*. New York: Revell, 1894 (rev. ed.).

2 China's Transitional Century, 1850-1950

C. Martin Wilbur

THE CENTURY before 1950 is the "living past" of the Chinese people. The attitudes of the present adult population and the ideas of the leaders regarding national goals and governmental policies were largely formed during the last few decades of that period. To understand why China is ruled by a Communist regime and why its leaders act as they do, we must observe the revolutionary process running through the preceding century.

From Troubled Empire To Faltering Revolution

Certain crucial problems emerged during the nineteenth century, and the Chinese nation has been struggling ever since to find solutions to them. Probably the most fundamental is the size of the Chinese population. During a century and a half of internal peace from 1700 to 1850, the population grew from about 135,000,000 to more than 400,000,000. This largest concentration of people in the world was accommodated by the reclamation and intensive cultivation of nearly every acre of possible farmland, by the growth of cities, towns, manufacturing and trade, and by migration into the deserts, mountains and forests around China's borders. The economy did not develop rapidly enough to care for this huge population, and neither governmental policy nor social ideology was adequate to assure a fair distribution. The results were social unrest and disorders, which by 1850 erupted into a series of rebellions. One of these, the civil war that we know as the Taiping Rebellion (1850-1866), was the most devastating war in the world during the nineteenth century. After nearly three decades of fighting, government forces were able to quell the various rebellions. Economic life was badly disrupted, and millions had died of war and famine. But after recovery the population began to grow as before. There was now almost no new land available, and China did not go through a technological revolution like the Industrial Revolution in Western Europe.

A second major problem lay in China's foreign relations. In essence, the issue was whether China or the Western world was to regulate their relations. Was the Manchu-Chinese state to enforce a traditional system of isolating foreign nations from China and keeping their represent-

CHINA'S CENTURY, 1850-1950

atives subservient, or were the dynamic nations of Europe, which were seeking trade and seizing colonies all over the world, to call the tune?

After about 1820 Western merchants were no longer willing to be restricted to a single Chinese port and forced to trade under archaic regulations. The first Anglo-Chinese war (1839-1842), though sparked by the conflict over opium, was also fought over the larger issue of the Manchu government's determination to regulate foreign trade according to its prevailing anticommercial philosophy as against the British determination to break down the obstacles to freedom of trade. China lost that war decisively.

The Western intrusion was helped by treaties, forced on China, which promised the protection of traders, officials and missionaries in their work. By the end of the century, the Manchu-Chinese Empire was beginning to lose its dependencies. The effort of France to detach present-day North Vietnam led to a war in 1884-1885, while a similar effort by Japan to detach Korea led to the Sino-Japanese war of 1894-1895. China was repeatedly humbled in the conflicts from 1840 to 1895.

No great and proud people will passively accept repeated humiliations. After each defeat, responsible officials tried hard to acquire the technology necessary to match Western military power. Meanwhile, Western merchants were settling down in China's major ports and missionaries were moving inland. Here and there, foreigners established little outposts of European culture, in addition to building chapels and churches, and establishing schools, hospitals and publishing houses. These two trends—China's efforts toward self-strengthening and the penetration of Western culture—had important social consequences. Educated Chinese began to learn about Europe and America. They began to talk of science, people's rights and parliaments.

China's swift and humiliating defeat by Japan in 1894-1895 led to reform efforts from above. Younger officials persuaded the youthful Manchu Emperor to modernize his government by decree. This effort was quashed by the Empress Dowager, who led a conservative reaction that opened the way for the antiforeignism of the Boxer Uprising of 1900. This attempt to solve the problem of foreign relations by killing or expelling foreigners led to a damaging war in which Peking was invaded by the troops of eight nations. After that came another burst of reforms, this time managed by the conservative Dowager Empress herself in a bid to save the tottering dynasty.

Modern China was greatly influenced by the fifteen years of reform-reaction-reform between 1895 and 1910. Thousands of students went to foreign countries, principally to Japan, to learn the skills of the modern world in science, medicine, engineering, law, education and military organization. Later, as "returned students," they became a modernizing force in society: the teachers, journalists, engineers, bankers, entrepreneurs, officials and military officers of the republican period. During their impressionable years abroad, some of these future leaders had absorbed a variety of un-Chinese social philosophies, such as the eighteenth century doctrines of republicanism and democracy, nineteenth century social Darwinism and concepts of national patriotism, and even radical doctrines of socialism and anarchism. China's present leaders, men such as Mao Tse-tung and Chou En-lai, were strongly influenced by the teaching and writing of the radicals among these returned students.

Another strong influence from this period was the revolutionary movement of which Dr. Sun Yat-sen was one of the leaders. The revolutionists considered the Manchu Dynasty the major obstacle to the nation's progress. Their aim was a republic in place of the imperial system that had ruled China for two thousand years. Finally a half-baked revolt that started unexpectedly in a provincial capital became a successful revolution, partly through support of the discouraged reformers but mainly through the manipulations of Yuan Shih-k'ai.

Yuan Shih-k'ai had been one of the last great imperial officials and the creator of China's most powerful modern military force. The Manchu court called him out of retirement to suppress the revolt, but Yuan had plans of his own. He used the power of the Peiyang Army, his influence in the bureaucracy and his prestige among the foreign powers to force the abdication of the Manchu Dynasty in favor of a republic and to persuade the revolutionaries to join with him in setting up a republic, of which he would be the first president.

An experiment with parliamentary government ended in less than two years when Yuan, an autocrat by training and career experience, expelled his opposition and began preparations to set himself up as Emperor. This project was interrupted by an ominous development. With the outbreak of World War I in Europe, Japan quickly joined the side of the Allies and seized German colonial possessions in Shantung, a coastal province of China. In March, 1915, Japan secretly presented to Yuan Shih-k'ai "21 Demands," which would make China virtually Japan's protectorate. Chinese patriots opposed the demands by propaganda, demonstrations and boycotts. Finally on May 7, 1915, Japan presented a 48-hour ultimatum to Yuan, requiring him to accept the terms as they stood at that point in the negotiations. When Yuan Shih-k'ai resumed his plan to make himself Emperor he ran into determined opposition and had to back away from his dream.

Political disintegration and the extension of Japanese power continued as major trends of the next decades. After Yuan's death China moved into the period of "warlordism." There was now no single strong ruler or regime to combine control of the military forces, the civil bureaucracy and the central government finances. Instead there emerged many military-political factions, each controlling a region, a province or even a few counties. The government at Peking became the tool of whatever faction dominated the North, but regimes in the West and South (such as one organized by Dr. Sun Yat-sen in Canton in 1917) simply disregarded its orders or protected their autonomy by alliances and defensive wars.

About 1917 an "intellectual revolution" began to take shape. A group of returned students now teaching in universities and editing journals were disillusioned with the anti-Manchu revolution, which had resulted in near anarchy. They searched more deeply into Chinese civilization for the roots of China's weakness. Influenced by reformist or radical social philosophies while studying abroad, some of them recommended far-reaching changes in China's ethical system and social institutions, the reform of the language and an attack on an economic system that permitted impoverishment of the masses. Students in the recently created modern middle schools and colleges were deeply influenced by these returned students. They were ardently patriotic and idealistic, and saw themselves as the conscience of the nation. Most of the present rulers of China came from this generation.

An incident that occurred on May 4, 1919, has given a name to the larger intellectual revolution. Patriotic students in Peking staged a parade to protest the decision of the Versailles Conference that Japan should retain defeated Germany's rights and possessions in Shantung Province. Waves of protest spread throughout the major cities of China. The government in Peking was forced to dismiss some officials charged with being tools of Japan, and to refuse to sign the Versailles Treaty. The popularity of the patriotic movement helped to spread the iconoclastic and reformist ideas of the broader intellectual movement, which was dubbed "The May Fourth Movement." By the early 1920's China was launched on a new revolutionary path.

Nationalists and Communists, 1920–1937

This new revolution, which came to be termed a "National Revolution," was led by the Nationalist party (Kuomintang) and the Communist party (Kungch'antang). The Nationalist party had its origins in the earlier revolutionary alliance against the Manchus. The patriotic upsurge of 1919 stimulated Dr. Sun Yat-sen and a small group of veterans to rejuvenate the Kuomintang. The Chinese Communist party grew directly from the May Fourth Movement. Its leaders and first members were professors and students of Peking University and other institutions, who came to believe that China must undergo a social revolution and who began to see

CHINA'S CENTURY, 1850-1950

Soviet Russia and its 1917 revolution as a model for China.

Russia's revolutionary leaders tried to court the goodwill of China by promising to abandon all the special rights that tsarist Russia had gained there in the past. Russia had also set up an international Communist organization, the Comintern, which in 1920 sent a few missionaries to China to see what could be done to organize a Communist party there. Thus, one may say of the origins of the Chinese Communist party that the soil was ready and the seeds had been planted before the foreign gardeners came. The small group that founded the Chinese party during 1920 and 1921 consisted of the more radical fringe of the patriotic reformist movement. Most were returned students, and a few were followers of Sun Yat-sen.

From 1923 to 1927, the Nationalist and the Communist parties cooperated in the National Revolution, whose aims were to reunify China, end the Unequal Treaty system and set the nation on a course of modernization and social justice. Soviet Russia encouraged this cooperation and supported the revolution with money, arms and advisers. This aid was part of a long-range strategy, by which Russia's leaders intended to bring China into the "world revolutionary camp."

Sun Yat-sen regarded himself and his party as the rightful leaders of revolution. He was sympathetic with the Russian revolution and eager to receive—and monopolize—Russian aid, and some of his followers had helped to found the Communist party. These were some of the reasons why he agreed in 1922 to allow members of the infant Communist party to join the Kuomintang, and why the Kuomintang drew close to Soviet Russia. The Nationalist leaders expected to dominate a partnership in which the Communist party would be a junior member.

The immediate goals of the National Revolution were the unification of China and the ending of the Unequal Treaties. The two key slogans, "overthrow the militarists" and "down with imperialism," had an enormous public appeal.

By 1924 China was disastrously fragmented. Regions or provinces were ruled by military coalitions that levied taxes, conscripted soldiers, manufactured or purchased arms and appointed the civilian administrators. They fought one another in a series of civil wars. Sun Yat-sen in Canton presided over just such a regime. He and his colleagues had the difficult task of creating enough power in South China and enough sympathy throughout the country to overcome the stronger regimes that stood between Canton and the national capital, Peking. Although Dr. Sun died in 1925 before his dream was accomplished, the Nationalist and Communist coalition did a remarkable job, with massive Russian help, in building a base of military power.

The Kuomintang established a military academy near the city of Canton, to train young officers who were indoctrinated with revolutionary ideology and taught to be loyal to the party. Chiang Kai-shek was the Commandant of the Whampoa Academy. Among present-day Communist leaders in mainland China, three of the best known taught or studied there: Chou En-lai, who has been Prime Minister of the People's government since 1949; Ch'en Yi, the Foreign Minister; and Lin Piao, the man who commands China's armed forces and may become Mao Tse-tung's successor as principal ruler of China. All three participated actively in the National Revolution.

This National Revolution was a patriotic movement. Antiforeign slogans had great appeal because of the repeated humiliations—the psychic wound—that China had suffered in its eighty-year encounter with the Western powers and Japan, and because of the system of special privileges that foreign powers had acquired in China. Most foreigners enjoyed extraterritoriality; that is, they were subject to the laws and courts of their own countries, but not to China's. They might live in settlements or concession areas that were not under Chinese jurisdiction. In these various sanctuaries foreign businessmen were scarcely touched by Chinese taxes, and native products received practically no protection against foreign goods.

These privileges were codified in treaties and protected by foreign-controlled police forces, military units stationed in or near China, and warships that freely entered Chinese ports and patrolled the major navigable rivers. The privileges were not reciprocal for Chinese; hence the treaties that codified them were termed Unequal Treaties. The term was accurate. A vigorous foreign imperium flourished within China, rendering it, in Dr. Sun's words, a "semicolony." Nationalistic Chinese opposed this situation head-on.

The leaders of the National Revolution tried to broaden their base of support by organizing labor unions and farmers' associations, and by trying to control student organizations and the movement for women's rights. The Chinese Communists were particularly aggressive and successful in stimulating and operating these "mass movements," which grew rapidly to several million members by late 1926.

The increasing militancy of the Communist-controlled mass movements during the course of the revolution naturally created resistance among those being attacked—large landowners, local political bosses, factory owners and leaders of rival unions. Revolution engendered counterrevolution even in the Nationalist-held areas. Moreover, as the Communist party became increasingly powerful some of its leaders demanded a greater voice in shaping the policies of the alliance. They mounted propaganda attacks against those Kuomintang leaders they considered too conservative and tried to force them out of the Nationalist party. Even

Chiang Kai-shek, the Nationalist Commander in Chief, became the object of disguised attack. Nevertheless from mid-1926 to early 1927 the southern revolutionaries moved from victory to victory, until half of China was under their control.

With final victory on the horizon all the rivalries, conflicting ambitions and fundamental differences in ideology exposed themselves. The issue whether the more radical or the more conservative revolutionaries would control the political destiny of China came to a head when the southern armies reached Shanghai. That great city held the key to the resources of China's wealthiest provinces, was the center of industry, commerce and banking, and the focal point of foreign trade. It was the stronghold of the conservative wing of the Kuomintang and the center of native capitalism. But it was also headquarters for the Chinese Communist party and the place where it had most successfully organized labor unions and given them paramilitary units to enforce strikes. Shanghai was likewise the concentration point of Western commercial, industrial and missionary activity. The International Settlement and French Concessions were protected by foreign troops and warships. Here the Chinese anti-imperialist movement was certain to crash against determined foreign opposition. Thus, in the struggle between radical and conservative revolutionaries, where the radicals were indisputably backed by Russia, the conservatives might hope for help from Japan, Britain or the United States.

One of the turning points of modern Chinese political history was the break-up of the alliance between the Nationalists and the Communists between March and August, 1927. The Kuomintang, "purified" of its Communist members, became a socially conservative though still intensely nationalistic party. It created the National government of the Republic of China, which ruled from 1928 to 1949 and still governs Taiwan. The Communists, driven from the coalition, their control of mass movements wrested from them, turned to insurrection. When urban insurrections failed, some of their leaders began to develop military forces in hinterland bases. As the "Red Army" grew and "Soviet" bases expanded, the National government launched "extermination campaigns" to suppress them. For twenty-two years the Nationalists and Communists fought for the support of the Chinese people and the control of the country. We can divide the struggle into three phases.

During phase one, from 1928 to 1937, the National government worked to unify China politically, to modernize the country and to reassert China's position as a sovereign state. The government expended great efforts to create modern military power—China's century-old need—and used that power to suppress regional militarist rivals. By 1936 most rival regimes had been subdued or reduced to provincial scale, and the Red Armies had been driven from central China into the barren northwest. In Communist annals this retreat is celebrated as The Long March. Many of China's present leaders of the first and second echelon are survivors of that grueling retreat.

The Nationalists did much to create a modern government, a coherent monetary and banking system and improved taxation; to expand the public educational system; to develop a network of transportation and communication facilities; and to encourage industry and commerce. It was urban China that mainly benefited. Little was done to modernize agriculture or to ameliorate the conditions of the rural poor. Rural China contained more than 300,000,000 people living in hundreds of thousands of villages and hamlets spread over a continental territory. To eradicate disease, illiteracy, underemployment, exploitation and backward agricultural methods in such a huge population was a formidable task.

The National government had some success in reasserting China's sovereignty. Several concession areas were returned to Chinese control, and the foreign powers handed back to the government authority to fix foreign tariffs. But these gains were merely a token. The people were in a strongly nationalistic mood, determined to reverse foreign economic and political penetration of their land. Manchuria was a huge and rich area, which Japan was converting into a virtual colony. It was thus inevitable that Chinese nationalism should crash head-on with Japan's expansionism in Manchuria.

In 1931 a group of Japanese army officers set in motion a plan to compel their government to extend its power in Manchuria and prevent the Chinese Nationalists' reassertion of authority. Open conflict began with the carefully staged Mukden Incident on the night of September 17-18. From this the Japanese government was drawn, step by step, into the conquest of Manchuria and the creation there of a puppet regime known as Manchukuo. China, militarily weak and under a government that had only begun to unify the country after a decade of regional separatism, was unable to prevent Japan from seizing this vital area. From 1932 to 1935 Japan went on to further aggression, seizing territory bordering Manchuria and setting up more puppet regimes. This situation helps to explain why the National government devoted so much of its resources to building its army and air force, and why it insisted that the nation must be united in the face of the enemy. "Unity Before Resistance" became the slogan for a policy of warding off Japan's advance through negotiation and international pressure, while trying to suppress domestic opposition—particularly by the Communists—through military means.

Several factors combined to bring a gradual shift in this policy. Continued Japanese aggression aroused Chinese patriotism, particularly among intellectuals and students. The idea spread that China must cease internal fighting and turn all forces against Japan before it was too late. Moreover, the advance of Japan and the rise of Hitler brought reorientation in the policies of Russia. The Seventh Comintern Congress held in Moscow in the summer of 1935 formalized a new strategy for national Communist parties. In their several countries, they should work for a united front with other political parties and groups to oppose fascism. The Chinese Communist party was instructed to work for a "united front" with—instead of against—the Kuomintang, the National government and Chiang Kai-shek. The Nationalist leaders were finally induced to halt their military campaign against the Red Armies in the Northwest as a result of public opinion and the Sian Incident of December, 1936, in which Manchurian officers arrested Chiang and would not release him until he agreed to lead a united China against the foreign foe.

Invasion and Internal Truce, 1937–1945

The Sino-Japanese War of 1937-1945 profoundly influenced the future of both nations. It also marked phase two of the conflict between Nationalists and Communists.

Japanese expansionism in North China and rising Chinese patriotism finally collided in July, 1937, over an incident near Peking. The prestige of both nations quickly became committed, and they were soon locked in a war that ended in the devastation of both. As never before in modern history, the Chinese united against the foreign enemy. For about a year the Chinese armies fought stubbornly and with terrible losses to protect the coastal cities and railway lines, but they were forced to retreat into the hinterland. By the autumn of 1938 most of eastern China, the major ports and industrial cities and practically all the rail lines had been taken by the Japanese army. The National government withdrew a thousand miles westward, establishing the capital in Chungking, a river town in the rich but backward province of Szechwan.

Japan tried to bring the war to an end. First it tried to negotiate, then to bomb the Nationalist capital into submission and then to set up a rival "puppet" regime in Nanking. But the majority of the Chinese people, their government and their armies would not submit. For the next five years, from 1939 through 1943, the battle lines between Japanese and Nationalist Chinese forces changed very little.

During these years social and economic conditions in "Free China" deteriorated. Inflation grew worse year by year, until in the end it was nearly uncontrollable. Years of privation and frustration sapped the morale of the National government's officials and military officers. Factional politics and corruption revived. It is not

CHINA'S CENTURY, 1850-1950

easy to say to what extent the reasons for this deterioration lay in the Chinese social system itself, or in particular wartime factors, or in the decisions and actions of the leaders of the government, notably the President and Commander-in-Chief, Chiang Kai-shek.

The war had precisely the opposite effect for the Chinese Communist party. Its leaders had survived ten years of civil war and had developed a unity, camaraderie and sense of mission that was unmatched by any other group in China. They had learned how to mobilize the rural population and to fight guerrilla war. Their ideology glorified struggle for a new form of society, which they believed would eliminate the inequities and exploitations of the present and create a strong nation. They were ardent patriots and knew how to manipulate the symbols of nationalism.

When the war began, the Communist party numbered about 40,000, and its Red Army, renamed the Eighth Route Army, contained about 90,000 poorly equipped men. But its officers were battle-hardened veterans linked together by party loyalty. Their base in the Northwest was far from the major theaters of war. Operating within the general framework of the United front against Japan, the leaders of the Eighth Route Army could make excellent use of their experience in guerrilla warfare. They sent their columns into areas of North China which the Japanese army had overrun but lacked the manpower to control. There they developed interdependent relations with the peasants.

The Communist party revitalized itself through combat. By 1945 the party membership had grown to about 1,200,000. This membership underwent intensive and continuous indoctrination, and the leadership systematically purified the ranks by expelling the dissident, ineffective and unsubmissive. The Communist armies grew to nearly 1,000,000 men, backed by a militia of 2,000,000. These years had a profound effect on the party itself. Its leaders became ever more attuned to the realities of Chinese rural life, while the rank and file were mostly Chinese peasants.

During the Sino-Japanese War the veteran Communist leaders never lost sight of their main objective—the seizure of power throughout China in order to carry through a "Socialist" revolution. Inevitably there were innumerable clashes between the Communists and the Nationalists, and by the end of 1941, the two sides were as much on guard against each other as they were against Japan.

Japan's bombing of Pearl Harbor brought the United States into alliance with China. Great Britain, too, joined the Pacific war as its colonial possessions in Asia were attacked. This widening of the Sino-Japanese conflict lifted Chinese morale, but its other early effects were harmful. Free China became virtually isolated from the outside world; this intensified the inflationary trend. Chinese war planners anticipated massive American assistance, but it was two years before American resources and power could begin to be effective in that distant theater. Serious friction developed between the Chinese and American allies: the United States wished to strengthen China's ability to resist and to prepare Chinese armies to join in Japan's defeat, while each Chinese side—Nationalist and Communist—was bent on using the war to strengthen itself for a civil war they both anticipated.

The United States government deplored this conflict and was determined not to become involved in China's internal war. Yet its alliance against Japan was with the National government, which it had recognized since 1928 as the government of China. American financial and military assistance naturally went to the established government, but this tilted the balance of power between the Chinese contestants. American aid to the Nationalists naturally aroused the enmity of the Communists. Thus was the United States entangled in the fifteen-year-old Chinese political conflict. (Russia had recognized the National government since 1937, aided it against Japan, and formally renewed that position as late as the Sino-Soviet agreement of August 14, 1945, the day Japan surrendered.)

In 1944 and 1945, as the Pacific war neared its climax, some independent Chinese leaders tried to persuade the Nationalists and the Communists to reach a negotiated settlement that would spare the country from more fighting. The United States had the same objective. But no foreign power could make the decisions for such determined men as Chiang Kai-shek and his supporters on the one side, and Mao Tse-tung and his colleagues on the other.

In August, 1945, Japan surrendered and the Republic of China was one of the victors. Eight years of war and privation seemed at an end. President Chiang Kai-shek, who had led the War of Resistance, was a national hero. The Unequal Treaties had been ended by British and American decision in 1943. Extraterritoriality and foreign-controlled settlements in China were a thing of the past. China was to regain the lost territories of Formosa and Manchuria. China was recognized in the United Nations as one of the five great powers. But the Chinese faced grave problems of rehabilitation and recovery, compounded by the threat of civil war.

FULL CIVIL WAR: THE COMMUNIST VICTORY

Immediately on Japan's surrender, the National government and the Communist party each rushed to seize control of the eastern cities, railways, factories and mines, and to establish its own political authority wherever possible. The third phase of the struggle between the Kuomintang and the Kungch'antang had begun.

In this take-over contest the Communist party, though militarily weaker, had some advantages.

CHINA'S CENTURY, 1850-1950

The Eighth Route Army was already established in guerrilla bases throughout North China; it was much closer to Manchuria and to the North China cities than were the Nationalist forces. The Nationalists also had advantages. America was their ally. The United States had been re-equipping and retraining the National government's army and air force in Southwest China. By August, 1945, the Nationalist forces were superior in numbers and equipment. Furthermore the allied governments, including the Russian, specified that Japanese military forces in China should surrender to representatives of the National government. The United States helped its ally by airlifting the best Nationalist divisions into the vital Shanghai-Nanking area and to other important centers. The United States also sent 50,000 United States Marines to the Tientsin-Peking area to assist in the takeover of that region and to prevent the Russian army from extending its control southward from Manchuria, which it occupied in the last week of the war. Russia, however, obstructed the entry of Nationalist troops into Manchuria and assisted the Communist forces with arms surrendered there by Japan.

During the latter part of 1945 and most of 1946, the contest for control of China was dampened down, partly through the efforts of U.S. General George C. Marshall, sent by President Truman to assist the peace negotiations between the government and the Communist regime. But the mutual suspicions and hostilities of the Chinese antagonists ran very deep. Their ideologies and political ambitions were irreconcilable. Furthermore, each side was reaching its peak of military power. Each was striving to win control over Manchuria, China's richest industrial region. By January, 1947, General Marshall realized that both sides were determined to settle the issue by arms and it was beyond the power of the United States to prevent civil war.

When the war really got underway, the National government had regained most of the territory that Japan had held south of the Great Wall. But its army in North China was now in the position where the Japanese army had found itself during the later stages of the war, holding major cities and railways while surrounded by enemy guerrilla bases.

A highly significant factor was the contrast between the unity and morale of the Communist leaders and the factionalism and self-seeking among Nationalist leaders. In the latter stages of the war against Japan, regional armies had begun to reassert themselves. After the government moved from the West back to the Shanghai-Nanking area, regimes in more distant provinces began to display some autonomy. In short, the Nationalist political system was unstable and its unity somewhat fictitious.

In traditional Chinese bureaucratic life there was a persistent tendency for some officials, perhaps most of them, to profit from office. The

Communist leadership had guarded the party very strictly from the rot of corruption in the government. During the confused period when the government took over the Japanese-occupied territories, in which were China's richest cities, some officials enriched themselves by seizing enemy supplies or extorting protection money from suspected collaborators. Inflationary pressures continued strong. Goods were short, transportation disrupted, factories producing at a low level. The government lacked the means through taxing and borrowing to raise the funds necessary to conduct civil war. It continued to turn out great amounts of paper currency, which could scarcely keep abreast of the decline in its value. This was disastrous to morale.

Propaganda and subversion played an important part in the war. Each side tried to eliminate enemy agents, but this was much harder for the city-based Nationalists than for the Communists. The battle for the allegiance of the Chinese people was fought in the schools, the press, the radio and the rumor market. Both sides tried to influence opinion abroad, particularly in the United States. Within the area under their own control, the Communist leadership reinstituted rural class war, setting in motion a land revolution in which landlords were killed or driven away and their fields distributed among the landless. The civil war was to be made a "people's war."

These political, economic and moral factors

influenced the outcome of the conflict, but the decisive events occurred on the field of battle. During 1948 the tide of battle turned in favor of the People's Liberation Army, greatly enlarged by consolidation of the experienced guerrillas in North China. The first decisive victory was in Manchuria, where the Fourth Field Army under Lin Piao began a sustained offensive against some of the best-equipped Nationalist armies defending important cities. Lin Piao's army cut up the Nationalists' supply lines and systematically destroyed outlying defense units, until by the autumn of 1948 the Nationalist divisions were divided and isolated in their fortresses. Mukden, the last important stronghold, fell to Lin Piao on November 1. The government paid the high price of between three and four hundred thousand troops and mountains of equipment for the attempt to take Manchuria before having established control over North China. Almost simultaneously, the government suffered another colossal defeat in the Huai-Hai Battle around Hsuchow, some 150 miles north of Nanking, in November and December, 1948. In this battle the government lost an additional half a million men. Thus in the last four months of 1948, the government lost half its best troops with their American equipment. Tientsin and Peking were now isolated and surrounded by Lin Piao's troops, which had moved southward after victory in Manchuria.

At this moment, in January, 1949, when Manchuria and North China had been lost and the Yangtze Valley lay exposed to the now superior enemy, President Chiang Kai-shek announced his retirement, leaving the problems of government and defence to an old rival, General Li Tsung-jen. But President Chiang only pretended to retire. He had withdrawn the government's gold reserves to Taiwan, made that island the base for the navy and air force and continued to give secret orders to the commanders of the remaining army groups.

In about a year from the capture of Mukden and Hsuchow, the People's Liberation Army went on to take Nanking, the Nationalist capital, on April 23, 1949; the Wu-Han cities and Shanghai in May, and Canton in October; then the government's wartime capital in Szechwan on November 30; and Chengtu, the Nationalists' last mainland capital, on December 27. A leading Chinese military historian has tersely concluded that the Nationalist Army was "betrayed from within by corruption, maladministration, and dissension in high places." The person most responsible was the President and Commander in Chief. By the end of 1949 the Nationalists held only Taiwan, Hainan and a few offshore islands, while the mainland was under control of the Chinese Communist party and its two creations, the People's Liberation Army and the newly established government of the

Chinese People's Republic. The long struggle for power was over.

Looking back at the half-century of political turmoil from the Boxer Uprising to the founding of the Chinese People's Republic, one can understand that the people who actually experienced that turmoil looked forward with relief to the prospect of peace and unity under a strong government. Remembering the persistent attempts of reformers to remedy China's many social problems—illiteracy, disease and poverty; the disfranchised position of women; the overcrowding of the land and interclass conflict in agrarian China, to name only a few—one senses the expectancy with which the educated regarded a party that claimed to know how to cure these ills and a new government that promised to work vigorously to do so.

The men and women who came to power in 1949 were part of that student generation active in the May Fourth Movement, at war with Chinese society and its ethical system. In psychological terms the individuals might be considered at war with themselves: trying to reject the very ethical code, Confucianism, that had shaped their personality structures. Among this generation some had found a new orthodoxy in the teachings of Marx and Lenin and a new focus for loyalty in the Chinese Communist party. Like other patriotic youth of their generation, they joined in a National Revolution to "save

China" but were unusual in a passionate identification with their party and a faith in a particular ideology. They were "true believers."

When the Russian strategy that directed the Chinese Communist party to work within the Kuomintang collapsed in 1927, the more militant "went into the wilderness" and for twenty-two years devoted their entire energy to building the independent power of their party through revolutionary work. They emerged as men and women in their fifties or early sixties, triumphant and full of confidence.

Half a lifetime in the party and two decades of work among the Chinese peasants left their stamp on China's new leaders. Their formal education had ended in the 1920's. For twenty years most of them had been out of touch with urban China and with the outer world. As revolutionists, their intellectual fare had been almost exclusively the classics of Marxism and the writings of their own principal theorist, Mao Tse-tung. They were doctrinaire and limited in their knowledge of the modern world.

Yet their doctrine had been tested and refined by experience. For these were leaders who had come to the top by their proven ability as strategists of revolution, as military commanders, as persuaders and mobilizers and as administrators. Unlike the leaders of any other Communist party that has seized power and been faced with governing a country, these men and women had years of experience in practical affairs. Yet this experience was largely confined to rural China. They had lived with the peasants, learned their woes and acquired some of their values. This was remaking in a Chinese mold. A group of "intelligentsia," most of whom had come from gentry or bourgeois homes and whose higher education had been acquired in westernized schools, had been absorbed back into the China least affected by the century-long influences of the Western world.

China, in short, was under the control of a group of its sons who were the product of a unique experience. They had hammered out a body of doctrine, a strategy of revolution and a vision of the future to which they all subscribed. They had fashioned more powerful instruments for remaking the nation than had ever existed before. First among these instruments was the unified Communist party, some 5,000,000 disciplined members effectively directed by themselves. This party permeated and controlled all the existing means of persuasion, coercion and administration: an army at the peak of efficiency and with no significant remaining opposition; an extensive secret police; mass organizations to mobilize and manipulate each social group in the population; all media of information and propaganda such as radio, press, and education; and an administrative bureaucracy controlled at all levels by party cadres.

3 People's Republic of China, 1949-1968

Theodore H. E. Chen

For THE Chinese Communist regime, 1958 was a banner year. As the regime approached the end of its first decade, its leaders were proud of its achievements and confident of its future. Foreign visitors were impressed with what they saw: wide streets, new buildings, clean depots, cities cleared of debris and beggars. Inflation had been stopped and a foundation laid for a stable and expanding economy. New roads, new irrigation works and new schools were being constructed. A promising start had been made in industrialization.

Strong Lights, Deep Shadows

The exultant mood of the Chinese Communists was reflected in the ambitious plans they announced in 1958. This was the year of the spectacular steel drive, the Great Leap Forward, and the "people's communes." The first Five-

Year Plan (1953-1957) had been completed. Production plans and quotas were fulfilled in agriculture and industry. The second Five-Year Plan was to be even more spectacular than the first.

But the grandiose plans of 1958 remained largely on paper. The promise of "more, faster, better and more economical" production by farms and factories was unfulfilled. In 1968, the mood of the Chinese Communist leaders was markedly different from that of 1958. Unity was shattered at the top by a severe power struggle and the exposure of deep-seated dissensions within the party hierarchy. Mao Tse-tung and his followers admitted the existence of strong opposition within the party. While propaganda focused its attack on "a handful" of dissenters, the Maoists on other occasions admitted that the opposition could not be easily eliminated and even that they found themselves in the minority.

This breakdown of unity and discipline was not a sudden happening; it was symptomatic of a mounting crisis, which the Maoists for years tried to overcome, without much success. In the closing months of 1967, after a couple of years of "fierce struggle," the Maoists could claim firm control in only five provinces and two major cities, out of a total of twenty-eight administrative areas.

Foreign visitors saw a different scene in 1967-1968. Instead of dynamism and steady progress, they observed uncertainty and disruption, violence and near-anarchy. On top of mounting troubles at home, the Communists had suffered reverses in foreign relations. Their popularity abroad, evidenced at the Bandung Conference of 1955, had plummeted to a low level. A number of African states that had established friendly relations became openly hostile. Even among neighboring countries, goodwill gave way to antagonism.

Why the contrast? What accounts for the deterioration of authority and leadership in the course of a few years? Why did the new regime lose the momentum of progress that once won the admiration of people at home and abroad? Answers to such questions will shed light not only on the nature of communism, its strengths and weaknesses, but also on the nature of Chinese society, the political disposition of the Chinese people and the strength of China's old traditions and cultural heritage.

It may be helpful to think of the eighteen years of Communist rule in China in terms of major periods: a transitional period from 1949 to 1952; the first Five-Year Plan from 1953 to 1957; the Great Leap Forward and the communes of 1958, with the ensuing period of adjustment; and the campaign for Socialist education, which began in 1963, with the intensified Great Proletarian Cultural Revolution, which sputtered fire and fury and shook the nation from 1965 on.

From New Democracy to Socialist Transformation

The early period of transition consisted of two phases: an initial phase of moderation and a subsequent imposition of tight control and suppression of opposition. When the Communists came to power in 1949, they made an effort to allay the fear that communism would destroy much that people held dear. The regime was called the New Democracy, defined by Mao Tsetung as "a new type of bourgeois-democratic revolution" serving as transition to a later "proletarian-Socialist revolution." The New Democracy promised to encourage the growth of capitalism and give due protection to private enterprise and private ownership of property.

The aim of the New Democratic Revolution, Mao said, was the elimination of imperialism and feudalism. Most people in China could readily agree to this kind of revolution. Communism was soft-pedaled; even socialism, the prelude to communism, was declared unsuitable for China at this early stage of the revolution. Moreover, it was emphasized that the New Democracy would last a fairly long time; in Mao's words, this period "is by no means short." With such assurances, people felt relatively at ease.

In the Communist ideology, the revolution is called a proletarian revolution and its aim is the dictatorship of the proletariat. In the New Democracy, however, the Communists recognized the role of nonproletarian classes. The "coalition" was supposed to consist of four major classes of people: the workers, the peasants, the *petite bourgeoisie* and the national *bourgeoisie*, with the workers in the leading position. The *petite bourgeoisie* referred to the intelligentsia, the handicraftsmen, the professional people, employees of business organizations and government offices. The national *bourgeoisie* consisted of capitalists willing to offer their services and assets to the new state. Mao Tse-tung called the national *bourgeoisie* "a comparatively good ally" who could be utilized "at a certain period and under certain circumstances." Despite this explicit warning that their acceptance in the new society was only temporary, the capitalists and urban *bourgeoisie* felt relieved that they would not suffer immediate loss of their position and assets.

The initial period of milk and honey did not last long. China's entrance into the Korean War in the autumn of 1950 was used to justify stern measures to stamp out all opposition and resistance. A series of laws and decrees were issued to suppress and punish different categories of "counterrevolutionaries." Mass trials and the public execution of hundreds of thousands of victims marked the progress of the "campaign for the suppression of counterrevolutionaries."

Other nationwide campaigns equally basic to Communist ideology and policy were launched after the Korean War. Referring to the twin objectives of defeating feudalism and defeating imperialism, Communist spokesmen explained that the agrarian reform was essentially a campaign to eliminate the landlords as a feudal class; while the Resist-America Aid-Korea Campaign was necessary to overcome American imperialism and its pervasive influences in Chinese society. At the same time, the campaign for ideological remolding, especially of China's intellectuals, was also directed at the elimination of patterns of thought and behavior considered incompatible with the Communist way of life and attributed to American or bourgeois influence—for example, individualism, liberalism, indifference to class struggle and concern for professional or occupational interests divorced from politics. It was the aim of "thought reform" to weed out these ideas and attitudes and to implant a new "proletarian" ideology. By these campaigns the regime strengthened its control over various sectors of the population.

Communist leaders had openly declared that the primary aim of the agrarian reform was not to relieve the poverty of the peasants, but to carry on a resolute class war against the landlords. The land and assets of landlords were requisitioned; numerous landlords were executed. By 1951, the landlords had been stripped of their position and influence, and the Communists were ready to turn to the urban *bourgeoisie*.

The prelude to an organized class struggle

against the urban *bourgeoisie* was the "three-anti campaign" of 1951. Originally directed against the three evils of corruption, waste and bureaucratism in party and government, the campaign soon shifted its direction and merged into the "five-anti campaign." Maintaining that the "three evils" had been fostered by the intrigue and enticement of the *bourgeoisie*, the Communists declared that it was necessary to attack the source of the evils: bribery, tax evasion, fraud, theft of state assets and leakage of state economic secrets. Investigation teams were organized to expose the guilt of well-known business people and to extract confessions, which became the basis of punishments. Employees were encouraged to press charges against their employers, wives to inform against their husbands and young people to denounce their parents for committing one or more of the five offenses. As in the agrarian reform and the anti-counter-revolutionary campaign, the methods of mass trials and public executions were used.

Punishment ranged from heavy fines to public humiliation and death by execution. Many chose suicide. This was a period of terror on the Chinese mainland. Millions of people met with tragic death. Many more were reduced to poverty, suffered physical and mental exhaustion or were sentenced to hard labor. For the Communists, the campaigns were considered a success because they silenced opposition and tightened the control of the state. The population was left with no doubt that the regime would destroy all resistance to its plans and policies. After the terrorism, it was easier to "persuade" the population to submit.

The first Five-Year Plan was launched in 1953. In that year, too, the Communists decided that time was ripe for terminating the New Democracy and inaugurating the era of socialism, which is a prelude to communism. The success of the various "mass campaigns" had proved the ability of the regime to "mobilize" the masses and obtain their submission by persuasion or coercion. The attack on landlords and the *bourgeoisie* had overthrown the traditional seats of power in rural and urban society. New "mass organizations" such as youth groups, women's federations, trade unions and comparable bodies for other segments of the population had been placed under the direct supervision and manipulation of the Communist party. The Five-Year Plan presupposes centralized planning, which is effective to the degree that the party-state can control and directly utilize all available material and human resources.

By 1953, the Communists believed that they had the country under firm control. The government structure set up in 1949 was intended to be temporary. The Communists were not then able to exercise power over the whole country, and they did not consider conditions favorable for elections. In lieu of a constitution, the new regime had adopted a "Common Program," which was a statement of the basic guidelines of government policy. Now, after four years, the Communists felt that they had sufficiently "consolidated" their power to take a few big steps in the direction of their goal.

Elections were held in 1954. A single slate was presented to the electorate. The principle of universal suffrage was declared, but persons classed as reformed landlords, counterrevolutionaries and some other bad elements were not allowed to vote. According to the electoral law, the people vote directly for deputies to the local congresses. But manipulation by party leaders is facilitated through a series of indirect elections to higher levels: the local congresses send deputies to the county congress, and similarly up through the provincial congresses to the national. The first National People's Congress, convened in 1954, elected Mao Tse-tung Chairman of the People's Republic of China, and Chou En-lai the Premier. The second National People's Congress, elected in 1959, made Liu Shao-ch'i the Chairman of the Republic, while Chou En-lai continued as Premier. Mao Tse-tung had no government office but retained his position as Chairman of the Central Committee of the Chinese Communist party.

All the appearances of representative government are structurally provided, but there is no surrender of power on the part of the Communists. Theoretically, the government officials on any given level are responsible to the congress that elects them; but they have the authority to decide when and whether the congress should be called to a session. Elections may be postponed, and have been, at the discretion of the government leaders. The Constitution, adopted by the first National People's Congress in 1954, provides that the decisions of the lower congresses are subject to the approval of the next higher congress, and the actions of all government officials are subject to the approval of the governing body of the next higher administrative unit. This is called democratic centralism and ensures the effective concentration of power at the top. The Communist party is the source of power and authority. It lays down the basic policies, and the government carries them out. Even though holding no government position, Mao Tse-tung remains the most powerful man in mainland China. Until he was denounced as the "top man in power taking the capitalist road," Liu Shao-ch'i was generally recognized as Mao's heir apparent. Chou En-lai remains as head of the bureaucracy.

The Communist party itself is organized on the same revered principle of democratic centralism. Delegates from local party organizations elect representatives to congresses, culminating in the National Party Congress, theoretically the highest body. Actual authority is exercised by the Central Committee, which in turn elects a Political Bureau (Politburo) of fifteen to twenty people, acting when the Central Committee is not in session. Official documents and policy statements are issued in the name of the Central Committee.

The Communist party extends its pervasive power into every realm of life. In every government or business office, in every village or urban neighborhood, in every factory, every school, there is a resident party representative—or committee—acting as the authoritative voice of the party. He is often referred to as the "leadership." Students, teachers, peasants, workers, all are expected to accept without question the leadership of the Communist party.

The first Five-Year Plan was molded according to the Communist ideology. Accent was laid on heavy industry and "Socialist construction." The old sectors of the economy were to be "remolded" into Socialist enterprises. Land given to the peasants during the agrarian reform was gradually taken away from its new owners. First, management was transferred to cooperatives; then ownership was passed on to collectives. Private industry and commerce as well as handicrafts also underwent the process of "Socialist transformation." These changes seemed to have been made without much opposition, and foreign observers praised the ingenuity of the Chinese Communists and their ability to achieve collectivization without the bloodshed and violent upheaval that Stalin brought to Russia.

Material progress was evident everywhere.

Production rose. The prestige of the new regime soared at home and abroad, and its stability and popularity reached a high point in 1957-1958.

RADICAL COMMUNISM STUMBLES

The success of the 1950's seemed to have intoxicated the Communists. They were overconfident of their ability to mold and remold the economy, the social structure and the entire population of China. In a hurry to reach their final goal, the Communists decided to establish communes as a step beyond the collectives. Just as the collective, with some two hundred households participating, was larger than the cooperative of twenty to fifty households, so the commune would encompass a whole area or entire township and would control the activities of 20,000 to 50,000 people. Moreover, the commune was not meant to be an economic unit only. It was introduced as a new social-economic-political-cultural organization regulating life in five major areas: agriculture, industry, trading, education and defense. Each person in the commune was to be concurrently a farmer, a worker, a student and a member of the militia. Collective living was to be practiced in public mess halls, public nurseries for the care of infants and service centers for sewing, mending, laundry and other household needs. In early summer, 1958, Chinese writers triumphantly declared that China was about to advance from socialism to communism.

The idea was attractive, but it did not work. From the ideological point of view, the Chinese Communists found themselves out of step with the rest of the Communist world. Khrushchev pointedly stated that the building of socialism was still the task of this day and that no country had made sufficient progress in socialism to advance to communism. From the practical point of view, the communes met with resistance from the people, and it has now been revealed that Mao's own colleagues among the top party hierarchy counseled against the rash experiment.

Unfortunately for the Communists, other factors conspired to compound their difficulties. Natural calamities seriously affected the crops and food supply. Open antagonism against the USSR led to a hasty withdrawal of Soviet advisers who had played an important role in key projects of industrialization. These events combined with the decline of morale to bring about serious economic dislocations, with the result that the Great Leap Forward turned into a dangerous slide backward.

Some Communist leaders, to their credit, saw what was happening and were realistic enough to adopt remedial measures in defiance of ideological dogmas. They greatly toned down the commune program and decentralized its administration to the extent that the actual working unit was no bigger than the agricultural producers' cooperatives of the past. They offered material incentives and unabashedly made an un-Marxist appeal to the profit motive of individuals. They even amended the process of land collectivization by allowing peasants to have small private lots for cultivation, with the privilege of selling what they produced. Thus they were able to halt the rapid deterioration of the economy and put it on the road to slow recovery.

Although the cutback of the Socialist drive actually saved the economy from disaster, the ideologues were alarmed by what they considered a dangerous reversion to capitalistic ways. They attacked the use of material incentives as "economism" and the advocates of such measures as "revisionists." As early as 1963, the Communists had launched a campaign for "Socialist education," with the purpose of sharpening and heightening the "ideological consciousness" of the people. Special stress was given to "class education," reemphasizing class consciousness and the class struggle.

The Great Proletarian Cultural Revolution is a continuation and intensification of the Socialist education campaign, with four major targets: those within the party who hold "revisionist" views; intellectuals who are unwilling to make a complete break with their past; young people who, despite Communist education and indoctrination, do not have firm ideological commitments; and the masses or the population in general, who have been slow to adopt the Communist way of life.

PEOPLE'S REPUBLIC, 1949-1968

The attack on revisionist elements in the Communist party has also become a power struggle for top leadership. Mao Tse-tung in his old age seems to have lost the realism that characterized the early years of his leadership. He dwells nostalgically on the early period of the revolution and the days of Yenan, when the rigors of life in the caves shut out any possibility of enjoyment and comfort. When he asks the Red Guards to "dare to destroy," he sounds very much like the radical revolutionary that he was forty years ago. He seems to be apprehensive that the revolution may change its direction and its essential character after his death.

Mao takes pride in his ideological insight and his interpretation of Marxism-Leninism. Infuriated by Liu Shao-ch'i's divergence from his major policy positions, Mao decided to denounce his long-time comrade and chosen successor and to gather around him a new coterie of followers who would accept *The Thought of Mao Tse-tung* as absolute guide.

The power struggle is fierce and relentless. But it is more than a grab for power by rival politicians. It is a fight between two schools of thought within the Communist camp, between ideologues who would follow dogmas (as enunciated by Mao) rigidly and blindly and the more realistic bureaucrats and technocrats who see the need of tempering the dogmas with recognition of actual circumstances. The realists do not reject the goals of socialism and communism, but they are willing to make temporary adjustments or take necessary detours.

It is now known that differences between the ideologues and the realists go back more than a decade to disputes over the speed of collectivization. When the communes ran into difficulties, the realists again raised their voices of dissent. We are now told that in 1959 the second National People's Congress elected Liu Shao-ch'i as Chairman of the Republic and chief of state not because, as announced at that time, Mao wanted to devote himself to ideological matters, but because he was forced out by dissenters who then held the majority in the Central Committee and the Politburo.

But there is something even more basic behind the dispute. What distinguishes the realists is not less commitment to socialism and collectivization, but more awareness of the practical difficulties involved in attaining them. The origin of their dissent lies in the attitude of the people, the resistance of the masses to the Communist program.

If this analysis is correct, the final aim of the Cultural Revolution is not simply to get rid of a few individuals, but to combat the ideas they hold and express. It attacks not only the revisionists, but the "revisionism" that persists in the minds of people—the intellectuals, the youth and the masses of China. The Cultural Revolution has, therefore, set out to destroy, in the words of the Red Guards' slogan, "old habits, old customs, old ideas, old culture."

According to the reasoning of the ideologues, the communes would have succeeded and the Great Leap Forward would not have failed if the people had been fully motivated by "proletarian ideology," if they had gotten rid of their "bourgeois" individualism and selfishness. But intellectuals have continued to hanker after the liberalism and freedom of bourgeois culture, young people still hold ambitions of personal advancement and personal success and the masses still look for material rewards.

A New Type of Man

What the ideologues demand is a new type of man, a new Socialist man who surrenders himself completely to collective good. When they set out to change habits, ideas and attitudes, they are actually taking up the gigantic task of remolding the hearts and minds of China's millions. In the first decade of their regime, the Communists were concerned with changing institutions, systems, things—and they had considerable success. By the end of the decade, the Communists came to realize that institutional changes do not go deep enough. The new systems and new institutions cannot succeed unless there is a new type of man to make them work. In the second decade of the Communist regime, the central problem is that of changing man.

In assessing Communist achievements in the first decade, observers have praised the organizational and administrative ability of the Communists. Besides, Communist propaganda was successful in presenting a cause and a challenge to the people. But an even more crucial element was the response of the people of China, known through the centuries of their history for their hard work and industry. They rallied to the call to build a strong nation and a better society. They toiled to increase farm production; they worked long hours in the factories; and their enthusiastic participation must be considered a major factor in the achievements of the 1950's.

Years of political instability before 1928 had deprived the Chinese people of an opportunity to contribute to national reconstruction by the use of their skills and their capacity for hard work. They were given this opportunity during a short period before World War II, when the stabilization of the Nationalist regime, after a period of disunity and warlordism, brought the nation such a relief that the people took up energetically the tasks of national reconstruction. They accomplished so much in the early 1930's that the world took notice of significant progress in road building, epidemic control, afforestation, agricultural improvement, educational growth and other areas of national life. Something of the same order took place in the 1950's. Enjoying peace and stability for the first time after a long devastating war, the people of China were diligent in the labors of national reconstruction. There was a release of energy and enthusiasm for positive achievement that looked like active support of the new regime.

Actually, the people were not responding to any political ideology. They did take pride in the fact that, under the positive leadership of a new government, the nation was overcoming the uncertainty and insecurity of the postwar years, and that an aggressive government seemed to be effectively asserting China's world position.

True, the terroristic campaigns and the class struggle had caused severe strain and tensions for all classes of people. By 1953, however, people were relieved that the worst was over.

The end of inflation was certainly a boon for all people. Such material changes as cleanliness in public places and the rise of factories and new opportunities for employment doubtless produced a pleasant anticipation of bigger things to come. The measures for labor insurance, old-age pensions and some provisions for the care of the aged, though on a small scale only, encouraged hopes for greater security in life.

Day in and day out, the people were told that a new day had arrived for the common man. Workers and peasants sat as representatives in councils of factories and were elected to congresses and other government bodies. Children of workers and peasants were given priority in admission to schools and universities. As a result of such material benefits and psychological uplift, people were willing to put up with such inconveniences as political indoctrination meetings, mass campaigns, shouting slogans and joining parades.

The basic trouble underlying the crisis and upheavals that have shaken the regime in its second decade is that the Communists and the people of China do not pursue the same goals. The people of China are mainly concerned with a better living in a peaceful society, and with a higher status of the nation in the family of nations. To the Communists, however, a stable economy and a strong nation are not the final goals. Their aim is to establish socialism and communism. The more energetically they press toward their ideological goals, the more they part company with the people of China—the intellectuals, the patriotic and idealistic youth and the practical-minded masses.

The separation became acute with the intensified drive for further collectivization and the communes. The peasants had submitted to the cooperatives and the collectives and surrendered their land ownership. But the commune demanded much more than the surrender of land ownership. It enforced a new way of life. The public mess halls and nurseries for infants meant drastic changes in family life, and the Chinese family is buttressed by strong sentiments and emotions that cannot easily be ignored. In the writer's opinion, at the bottom of the revisionist dispute in China is a recognition on the part of the more realistic Communist leaders that the people have become disenchanted with the regime and that it is necessary to adopt effective measures to check the deterioration of morale and to recapture the mass support and enthusiasm of earlier years.

Instead of recognizing the defects in their own program, the ideologues, with Mao as their leader, blame the people. The ubiquitous Red Book of the Red Guards, *Quotations from Chairman Mao Tse-tung*, contains numerous dictums and exhortations, which can be boiled down to one central theme: the new man must be utterly selfless and his whole life must be guided by one single ambition and determination—to serve the revolution under the direction of the Communist party.

The Cultural Revolution is being waged in fury because after seventeen years of indoctrination, propaganda and education, the ideologues find that old ideas and old attitudes still persist. The intellectuals of China, despite round after round of thought reform, are still intransigent. In 1957, taking advantage of a brief period of relaxed control marked by the slogan, "Let a hundred schools contend, let a hundred flowers blossom," the intellectuals burst out with a torrent of sharp criticisms against Communist policies and against the miscarriage of justice in the terrorist campaigns. So vehement were the attacks on the regime that it was necessary to silence them with an "anti-rightist" campaign. After 1958, the intellectuals became overtly restless again. Unable to publish direct criticism, they resorted to allegorical and satirical writings. Once more, the party-state had to marshal its forces against literary people, historians, philosophers and other intellectuals who had expressed "revisionist" views of one kind or another. The attacks on these intellectuals were really the first guns fired in the Great Proletarian Cultural Revolution.

The Communists have also been disappointed with youth. Too many young people are concerned about their own personal interests. Instead of accepting unquestioningly the tasks assigned to them by the party-state, many complain about placements made without regard for personal interests. Others are unhappy because they are far and long separated from their families. Still others want further study, when the party-state requires them to work in production or political activities. Such young people do not measure up to the standards of the new man. The Maoists moan that there are not enough young "revolutionary heirs" who are fit to take over the responsibility from the aging veterans.

The masses, too, are a long way from the Communist ideal. They expect rewards for hard work. They adhere to old traditions and old customs. They want more food, better housing and more comfortable living. These are bourgeois desires unworthy of the Socialist man. What the Maoists condemn as revisionism seems to be rampant in Chinese society.

The second decade in the People's Republic was highly unfortunate from all points of view. It is unfortunate for the Communists because they have slipped from the height of power they reached in the first decade of their regime. It is unfortunate for the people of China because they have toiled hard and suffered much and still they can see no early fulfillment of their hopes and dreams. If the Communists had continued their early program of economic reconstruction and nation-building, they might have kept up the momentum of progress of the first decade. Now, the question is how or whether they can recover the previous momentum. To do this, they would have to find some way to rekindle the enthusiasm and optimism of previous years. Can they do this?

Already the Cultural Revolution has caused great damage to the nation and the regime. Chou En-lai admits that the disruption of production has adversely affected the economy. No less serious is the destructive effect on education, by no means concluded. Schools and universities were closed for a whole year. Even at the time of writing, when schools are supposed to reopen and the Red Guards are ordered to return to the classroom, the educational situation is far from normal. The very order of the party-state to "return to the schools and wage revolution" suggests that the main consideration is to get the young people off the streets and halt their destructive activities, rather than to resume the normal processes of schooling.

The defiant action of local authorities may lead to the resurgence of provincialism and regionalism. If the army should play a key role in the restoration of order, the danger of warlordism may increase. For four decades, Mao has warned against factionalism and warlordism. The emergence of either will pose a threat to the party-state.

Psychologically, the people's image of Communist leaders has been tarnished by the charges hurled against erstwhile comrades in the power struggle. They no longer appear as a united and dedicated group, and they are losing their power to inspire confidence or fear.

The immediate future depends on the outcome of the power struggle. If Mao and his followers gain the upper hand, the hard-line policy of the ideologues will hold sway. Dogmas will lead them farther and farther away from the people, and it will be very difficult for the regime to recapture popular support and enthusiasm. If, on the other hand, the anti-Mao elements should win, the adoption of a more realistic policy will probably stimulate economic recovery, and the restlessness of the people may be mitigated. The revisionists might seek a mending of Sino-Soviet relations, and Communist China might return to the main camp of international communism.

There is a strong possibility that instead of a clear-cut victory for either Maoists or anti-Maoists, the present turmoil will continue for some time with no decisive solution of the issues. Temporary compromises may introduce periods of relative moderation in the intraparty struggle, but the basic conflicts will remain and new tensions are bound to disturb the social, economic and political life of the nation.

In the long-range view, the crucial question is whether Communists of either group can solve the "inner contradiction" between them and the people of China. Liu Shao-ch'i, now denounced as an arch revisionist, has long been an exponent of "Communist morality," which demands absolute subservience of the individual and the unconditional sacrifice of personal interests and welfare for the sake of the revolution. He and his followers, whom, for the sake of contrast, we now call realists, also attach great importance to the production of a new type of man—the Red expert, the collectivist, the selfless individual. They may employ milder methods, but they will still press the remolding of the hearts and minds of the intellectuals and the masses alike. Will they succeed?

The Communists seem to believe that man can be remolded and remade to fit their blueprint of a collectivist society. They seem to proceed from the premise that thoughts, attitudes and aspirations can be changed and redirected according to the desires of the planners. For example, they encouraged students to leave schools and join the roaming Red Guards; but when the rampaging youth went beyond the limits originally intended by the authorities, they ordered the young people back to the classroom, as if the emotions engendered in the riots and the power struggle could be turned on and off by simple directives.

They once mobilized millions of people in a campaign demanding the "liberation of Taiwan," but a little later, they called off the campaign without worry of contradiction. Once upon a time, vast resources of education and propaganda were utilized in a concerted effort to teach the Chinese people to "learn from the Soviet Union" and to pledge undying friendship for the USSR, but now the same media are used to vilify the leaders and the government of the USSR. Is it possible to manipulate human minds and hearts as if they were clay in the potter's hands?

4 China and the Chinese Among the Nations

Claude A. Buss

FROM TIME immemorial, the Chinese people have derived their greatest satisfaction from their families and the good earth. As heirs of a flourishing culture, they felt no need for the world beyond their horizons. The Middle Kingdom, as they called their country, was all that mattered. The élite, the educated civil servants who ran the country, looked on anything foreign with a mixture of scorn and indifference. They called foreigners "outside the country" people, people beyond the pale of Chinese cultural blessings. Foreigners inside China had no rights or privileges except those the Emperor condescended to grant.

PRINCIPLES AND TACTICS IN FOREIGN RELATIONS

The impact of the West shattered Chinese complacency. Almost against her will, China was opened to the modern world. For a century preceding the rise of the Communists to power, China was subjected to diplomatic and military humiliations that reduced her from the proudest and most glamorous of ancient cultural centers to the most underdeveloped and weakest of the modern nation-states. When the Communists took charge in Peking, they felt that they had a terrible score to even with history.

The Communist rulers, while dedicated to communism, inherited the traditionally Chinese outlook on world affairs. They admitted no basic contradictions between their concept of China's national interests and the demands of the international Communist revolution. They believed that anything that was good for one had to be good for the other. The thought of Mao Tsetung was relied on to adapt the principles of Marx and Lenin to the unique situation in China.

At the time the Communists came to power they paid closest attention to certain vital interests: security and territorial integrity, economic viability, enhanced prestige and the preservation of their chosen way of life. They also adopted the Communist dogma that Communists were the protagonists of the working classes and oppressed peoples everywhere, that armed struggle was the central and unavoidable process of revolution, that a basic, worldwide conflict between capitalists and Communists was inevitable and that ultimate victory could come to the Communists only after capitalism and imperialism were destroyed.

CHINA AMONG THE NATIONS 91

In 1949 they announced a "Common Program" to protect China's independence, freedom and integrity, to work for lasting peace and friendly cooperation between all countries, to unite the USSR and all Communist states against imperialists headed by the United States and to protect the overseas Chinese.

During their years in power, the Communist Chinese have not limited themselves to an inflexible line of action in pursuing their unchanging goals and objectives. Sharp variations in tactics distinguish four clearly marked periods in the implementation of their foreign policy. These periods are 1949-1954, 1954-1957, 1957-1965, and 1965 to the present.

In the first period the Communist Chinese, flushed by victory in civil war and by their creditable record in Korea, followed an uncompromisingly hard line. They showed no tolerance for neutrals in the world revolution. They declared that nations would have to lean to one side or the other. They relied on people's diplomacy more than on ordinary relations with established governments. They extended diplomatic recognition only to those countries that were willing to sever relations with Chiang Kai-shek.

During the second period, which began with the Geneva Conference on Indo-China in 1954 and ended with the International Conference of Communists in Moscow in 1957, Communist China stressed the theme of peaceful coexistence. The highlight of the period was the Bandung Conference of twenty-nine Afro-Asian states, where Chou En-lai stated publicly that he would negotiate with the United States any issue promising a reduction of tension in East Asia. During these years, China signed many treaties with other nations based on the five principles of: mutual respect for territorial integrity and sovereignty, nonaggression, noninterference in one another's internal affairs, equality and mutual benefit, and peaceful coexistence. She extended financial help and technical assistance to selected underdeveloped countries and undertook to settle boundary disputes.

In the third period, 1957 to 1965, Communist China veered back toward the hard line. She lost the image of peaceful coexistence when incidents on the border with India led to open hostilities in 1962. Cooperation with the Soviet Union gave way to conflict. The solidarity of the international Communist movement was shattered. Chinese assistance programs took on a more militaristic complexion, and propaganda against the "imperialists and their lackeys" became more vitriolic. Active support was promised for wars of national liberation everywhere, and the United States was branded more viciously as the common enemy of "the people."

In the fourth period, which began with the speech of Marshal Lin Piao on September 2, 1965, Communist China showed herself to be totally uncompromising in her determination to achieve her international objectives. Lin Piao argued that it would be impossible to settle peacefully the contradictions between the imperialist aggressors and the oppressed peoples. He warned that the imperialists might threaten the Chinese people by risking another large-scale ground action on the Asian mainland. He described the settlement of the issue by war not as a catastrophe but as the central task and highest form of the revolution. He expressed his faith in the inevitable triumph of people's wars all over the world. He affirmed Mao's theory that the cities could always be overthrown by attacks from the countryside. He likened the imperialist strongholds in North America and Western Europe to the "cities" of the world and the rural revolutionary areas in Asia, Africa and Latin America to the "countryside." China's hard line resulted in many diplomatic defeats and the loss of much international goodwill, but it satisfied the Peking government's urge to take a clear stand in defense of what it considered China's national interests and revolutionary principles. The Chinese people do not conceive of themselves as the enemy of the rest of the world or as a menace to peace.

Consolidation: The Close Neighbors

Communist China's major preoccupation is the strengthening of the home base: Taiwan, Tibet and Inner Asia. Taiwan is looked on as an inseparable part of China. In Peking's view, there is only one China, not two. Communist China seeks a secure frontier in Inner Asia, an objective that implies unquestioned control in Manchuria, Mongolia, Sinkiang and Tibet. China's problems in these areas are of two kinds: relations with indigenous peoples and the possibility of conflicts with the foreign powers beyond the frontier.

In Manchuria, the first objective is to guarantee the security of this rich land from any possible external menace. The naval bases, harbors, port facilities, farms and factories are entirely Chinese. Communist China, however, is very alert to the dangers to Manchuria inherent in the Russian economic development of Siberia and the Russian military establishment there. The border bristles with enemy soldiers. Communist China feels that someday the one-sided nineteenth century treaties, which gave Russia the maritime provinces and the northern watershed of the Amur River, should be rectified.

In Mongolia, racial animosities are more significant than in Manchuria. The Mongols are divided into the Russian-oriented Mongolian People's Republic (Outer Mongolia) and the Chinese Inner Mongolian Autonomous Region. The Mongols as a race harbor an historic animosity toward the Chinese, which complicates China's endeavors to maintain friendly relations with Outer Mongolia. The Chinese have extended substantial economic and technical assistance to Outer Mongolia, but in their programs they have been matched by the Russians.

In Chinese Turkestan, or Sinkiang, the Peking government has taken care to see that the different ethnic groups—Kazakh, Uzbek, Kirghiz and the like—do not try to unite with their kinfolk in Soviet Turkestan to form a single Turkic nation. The Peking government has established firm political control in Sinkiang and has effectively displaced Russian influence. She has undertaken economic development and immigration programs intended to bind Sinkiang closer to China proper. Communist China has accused the Soviet Union of stirring up trouble on the China side of the border and of carrying out provocative military maneuvers unreasonably close to Chinese territory.

Tibet has been Communist China's most difficult minority problem. The Tibetan way of life placed great emphasis on the Buddhist religion, the Dalai Lama and a feudalistic hierarchy of nobles and monks. China occupies Tibet with a large military garrison and relies on force to prevent an explosion of Tibetan nationalism. Peking has carried out an intensive policy of Sinification and has built strategic motor roads between Lhasa and western China. Tibet is essentially an occupied territory treated by Peking as part of its national domain, effectively removed from the arena of international politics. Among the reasons Peking gave for hostilities with India were the allegations that India had expressed sympathy with the Tibetan rebellion and had offered sanctuary for escaping rebels and for the Dalai Lama himself.

Although maps in Chinese schoolbooks show that Korea and Vietnam were once part of Chinese territory, the Peking government makes no effort to reassert its sovereignty over these countries. To Peking, North Korea represents all of Korea, and North Vietnam represents all of Vietnam. Just as the United States sees Communists—and particularly China—as the real enemy behind Korea and Vietnam, so Communist China sees "imperialist aggression headed by the United States" as the single force blocking the success of the "wars of liberation." Chinese fear of the United States far exceeds the American fear of China and accounts for at least a part of the fanaticism in the foreign and defense policies of Peking. Communist China is all too aware of the military might of the United States and the gap between their respective nuclear capabilities. The Chinese people see the American area of operations in Asia as being on their very doorstep, and they have been led to believe that the Americans would not hesitate to invade or to bomb China if the "American national interest" so required.

China's relations with Korea and Vietnam are dominated by considerations of security and the preservation of friendly regimes. The sense of direct threat to China's territory played a major part in China's decision to send her volunteers across the Yalu River in 1950. China, the Soviet

Union and North Korea presented a solid front against the United Nations during the hostilities and during the armistice negotiations. Since the armistice in 1953, Peking has played the major role in standing up against the United States at Panmunjom, and has followed along with the Russians in helping to rebuild North Korea. Communist China has concluded a mutual defense treaty with North Korea and has done her best to keep North Korea on the Chinese side of the Sino-Soviet ideological dispute. She wants North Korea's support in promoting wars of national liberation.

With regard to Vietnam, the Chinese have from the beginning recognized Ho Chi Minh as the president of all Vietnam. They gave Ho as much help as possible against the French and supported him during and after the Geneva Conference. The Chinese contributed to the industrialization of North Vietnam, looked with sympathy on Ho's land reform program and modernized the transportation system from China into Vietnam.

Since the fighting has broken out between the United States and North Vietnam, Communist China has been completely committed to Ho Chi Minh's victory. She sees the hostilities in Vietnam as an important part of "the world struggle against United States imperialism in defense of world peace." China may, at times, be suspicious of Hanoi's claim to leadership over the Communist parties in the rest of the Indo-

China peninsula, but China states repeatedly that she "will remain as close as lips to the teeth" in backing North Vietnam. China opposes peace negotiations and urges the Vietnamese to fight until the American aggressors are forced into "immediate, complete and unconditional withdrawal."

In Laos, Burma, Nepal, India and Pakistan, China has used every device—trade and aid, subversion and infiltration, psychological and military warfare—to keep the goodwill of friendly governments, to oppose unfriendly regimes and to counter the influence of the United States and her allies.

In Laos, Peking has supported independence and neutralism and has worked for the predominance of the Communist-inclined Pathet Lao. Throughout the civil wars, whomever the United States has endorsed, China has opposed. She has resumed diplomatic and consular relations with Laos. She has undertaken a road-building program linking Laos to China and completing the East-West highway system from Hanoi to the Thai border. China tolerates the neutralism of the Laos government for fear that the only possible alternative would be an American-dominated right-wing regime.

In Burma and Nepal, Chinese policies before the Great Proletarian Cultural Revolution were good examples of Chinese-style peaceful coexistence. Political and diplomatic relations were correct and state visits were frequent. Economic assistance programs were substantial and were enhanced by friendly propaganda. Boundary disputes were settled in a spirit of understanding. Since 1965 Peking has looked upon the regimes of Burma and Nepal as "enemies of the people" and has shifted from a policy of goodwill to one of hostility. The enthusiasm of the Red Guards inside China has led to incidents that have threatened to rupture diplomatic relations. Peking is far more concerned about indoctrinating her youth with the correct thought of Mao Tse-tung than she is about preserving a favorable diplomatic position in Rangoon or Katmandu.

In dealing with India, Communist China blows hot and cold. China recognizes India's potential greatness and shares the common sentiment that both are Asian and leading members of the underdeveloped world. China would like to see India go Communist and supports those Indian Communists who share Peking's ideological concepts. China appreciates the lingering anti-imperialism in India, but she also fears that India may inherit some of the ambition of former British rulers to expand her frontiers at the expense of China. She dislikes the way India has drawn closer to the United States and to the Soviet Union.

Before 1962 China and India stood together in their opposition to colonialism, military pacts and atomic weapons. New Delhi supported Communist China's claims to Taiwan and to entry into the United Nations, and Peking tolerated India's neutralism. In 1962 hostilities broke out because of alleged Indian interference in the Tibetan revolt and military incidents along the India-China frontier. Since then China has paid little deference to common interests in Asian solidarity and desire for renewed peaceful coexistence. Official representatives in both countries have been mistreated as China and India have drifted apart. No matter how far China goes in denouncing India, however, she always expresses a hope for good relations and leaves a way open for possible reconciliation.

China's attitudes and policies toward Pakistan are the reverse of those toward India. Since India has veered so unmistakably to the West, China has drawn closer to Pakistan. When convenient, China has chosen to ignore Pakistan's religious foundations and democratic proclivities. China does not expect exclusive favors from Pakistan. She only wants to keep Pakistan and India apart and to reverse, as far as possible, Pakistan's former ties with the West. Pakistan is the most favorable place to attack the American military alliance systems of the Middle East and Southeast Asia. What China loses with India in the subcontinent of Asia, she hopes to replace with Pakistan. In pursuit of these policies, China gives Pakistan complete endorsement in her views about Kashmir. China has come forward with economic assistance and has offered Pakistan an overall treaty of friendship.

CHINA AMONG THE NATIONS

In 1968, China could say with some justification that Pakistan was the country outside the Communist orbit with whom she enjoyed the best relations.

The Other Asian Neighbors

Cambodia, Malaysia and Singapore, Thailand, the Philippines and Indonesia are sufficiently close to China to be classed together as neighbors, though "more distant neighbors." Until 1967 Communist China extended to Cambodia and her chief of state, Prince Sihanouk, courteous and generous treatment. Peking was highly pleased with Cambodia's consistent attitude of standing up to the United States and to the Soviet Union. China supported Cambodia in her continuing feuds with South Vietnam and Thailand. Peking was pleased that Cambodia shared China's point of view in extending full support to Hanoi and the Vietcong in the Vietnam hostilities. In 1967, however, Communist China abandoned her traditional hands-off policy toward the overseas Chinese in Cambodia, and Prince Sihanouk accused the Peking government of supporting the local Communists who opposed his rule.

Communist China is circumspect in her dealings with Malaysia and Singapore, primarily because the skills and assets of the overseas Chinese are much too valuable to be sacrificed needlessly. Peking is suspicious of the lingering military power of the British bases in Malaysia and Singapore and fears that the Americans will replace the British when the British withdraw. Peking has never given the West cause to believe that she wishes to absorb the Malayan Peninsula in her own body politic. Communist China openly supports the underground antigovernment Malayan National Liberation League, whose program calls for "genuine independence, anti-imperialism and anti-militarism, democracy, progressive national economy, and improvement of the people's livelihood." Beyond her propaganda and clandestine activities, Peking is in no position to influence adversely the pro-Western governments of Tengku Abdul Rahman in Kuala Lumpur or Lee Kwan Yew in Singapore.

Communist China is inclined to dislike the prosperous, capitalistic Buddhist monarchy of Thailand and its militaristic government. Communist China knows that Thailand sided with Japan in World War II and fought with the United Nations against China in Korea. Her present government is bitterly anti-Communist and is reponsible for discriminatory legislation against the ethnic Chinese minority. Communist China would like to promote a war of national liberation in Thailand. A China-inspired radio, calling itself "the voice of the people of Thailand," broadcasts constant appeals to the Thai to "overthrow the government and expel the Americans." The Chinese have created a Thailand Independence Movement, backed by a Thai Patriotic Front sponsored by Thai exiles in China. In the eyes of Peking, Thailand is nothing more than a puppet of the United States in "aggressive imperialist" policies in Laos and Vietnam.

Peking wastes little sympathy on the Philippines, which is considered hopelessly un-Asian and pro-American. She sees the intensely Catholic Philippines as the most anti-Communist of all the Asian nations. Recently, however, Peking has taken a new look at the Philippines, with the reemergence of the Huks in central Luzon and the growth of anti-Americanism in Manila. Peking shies away from open intervention in Philippine internal affairs, but she spreads propaganda in praise of the "Philippine people's war" against the corrupt Philippine government. Recently, she has invited Philippine officials and journalists to China, and has made overtures in the direction of the establishment of trade relations. She has shown a cautious interest in Philippine students, labor unions, tenant and farmer associations and youth organizations. Peking is tolerant of the strong spirit of Philippine nationalism and seems to realize the impracticability of trying to woo the Philippine government from its pro-Western orientation.

Until 1965 Peking was highly content in her relationships with the Indonesian government under President Sukarno. Peking, and much of the rest of the world, felt that Indonesia would be the next domino to fall to the Communist side. In spite of racial prejudice against Chinese in Indonesia, Peking relied on Indonesia to constitute the advance base for Communist expansion throughout all Southeast Asia. Peking was particularly pleased when Sukarno told the United States "to go to hell with her aid" and pulled Indonesia out of the United Nations. In 1965 the cordial sentiments between Communist China and Indonesia were drowned in blood. On September 30, local Communists, allegedly backed by Peking, attempted a coup. In retaliation, ethnic Chinese were slaughtered by the ten thousands and life was made excessively difficult for those Chinese who remained in Indonesia. By 1968 Peking was obliged to look on the post-Sukarno pro-Western regime in Indonesia as a confirmed enemy.

Of all China's neighbors, Japan is considered potentially the greatest friend or foe. Japan is close to China and, to a large extent, shares with China a common cultural heritage. China appreciates Japan's strength. She is aware that Japan might shortly become the third greatest economic power in the world and that Japan has the industrial and scientific knowledge to build nuclear weapons anytime she chooses. China wishes to keep "economics and politics" separate when dealing with Japan, and seeks expanded trade and commercial credits. Japan is seen as a key source for outside technical assistance in China's program for modernization.

Nevertheless, Communist China remembers vividly the militaristic, aggressive Japan that crushed China under her heel in the 1930's and 1940's. Peking cannot erase the fear that Japan might again become a menace in Asia, especially with a conservative government in Tokyo whose policies are closely linked to those of the United States. Peking sees the new Japanese economic drive into Southeast Asia and the resumption of normal relations with South Korea as possible efforts to renew the "Greater East Asia Co-prosperity Sphere." China remembers Japan's cooperation with the forces of the United Nations in the Korean War and fears that Japan under a conservative government could again become, in concert with the United States, a serious menace.

In 1954, Communist China evidenced for the first time a willingness to normalize her relations with Japan. During the following decade she expanded her trade, promoted cultural contacts and arranged for the repatriation of the remaining Japanese nationals in China. Peking was galled by the unpleasant fact of Japanese subservience to the United States and the close relations between Japan and Taiwan. Peking had little use for Japanese Communists (whom she regarded as a colorless, spineless lot), and she lavished her attention on the Japanese left-wing Socialists.

Although Communist China is entirely conscious that the formal state of war with Japan has not been terminated, the constant theme of her propaganda is that the two countries should live together in friendship. Since China has demonstrated her nuclear capability, she wants Japan to adopt China's proposals for the complete prohibition of atomic weapons and the destruction of existing stockpiles. She wants Japan to enter into a collective security treaty for Asian nations and to do away with American bases on Japanese territory. She fears that "with the return of militarists and fascists to the control of the government, police and civil service, with the proliferation of secret societies and with the infiltration of ultranationalists into educational institutions and propaganda media, Japanese militarism is staging a comeback more powerful and more dangerous than ever before." In Peking's view the only way to offset these dangers is for Japan to become truly "independent, democratic, peaceful and neutral," so that China and Japan together can cooperate effectively for Asia's development and world peace.

The excesses of the Red Guards and the Great Proletarian Cultural Revolution have cost China dearly in Japan. As long as China concentrated on peaceful development and followed a low-key foreign policy, she won a great deal of sympathy in Japan, especially among the left-wing intellectuals. But China does not appear to be willing to tone down her revolutionary enthusiasm in order to satisfy Japanese critics or to allay the fears of Japanese sympathizers. Peking feels that Japan has as much need of China as China has of Japan.

Russia, the United States and the Outer World

Beyond the immediate Asian environment, China's concern for the success of the world revolution forces her to focus her attention on the Soviet Union and the United States.

China looks at the Soviet Union from two points of view: as a great nation-state and one of the world's two super-powers, and as the senior partner in the Socialist-Communist ideological camp. As a nation-state, China sees in the Soviet Union a bitter rival or a potential friend. At any given moment in history, she can be either one or a little of both. China is aware of inflammable points on the Russian-Chinese border, which is the longest in the world. The contest for influence continues among the Mongols and the Turkic peoples of Central Asia. The Chinese fear the possible extension of a Russian national interest beyond Vietnam into the rest of Southeast Asia. National rivalries in the past have taken Russia and China to the brink of war, and they could do so again. On the other hand, China and Russia have buried their differences in the past (1860, 1896, 1924, 1950) for their mutual advantage, and they could conceivably join forces again in the face of common danger.

These zigs and zags in ideological relationship are as old as the international Communist movement itself. Their differences seemed to be ironed out in 1950, when China and the Soviet Union signed a Treaty of Friendship, Alliance and Mutual Assistance. They gave the appearance of a monolithic team in promoting the world revolution. They cooperated for a decade, with only a minimum of manageable controversy. Since Khrushchev turned Russia toward peaceful coexistence with the West, China has denounced the Soviet Union for her "deviationism" and "revisionism." In the Chinese book, the Soviet Union is the blackest of criminals because she has failed to carry out her responsibilities as the leader of the Communist world.

Communist China accuses the Soviet Union primarily of abandoning her Chinese ally. When China needed Soviet technicians most, the Soviet government recalled them. The Soviet Union cancelled her assistance programs and caused critical delays in China's industrialization. China blames the Russians for becoming "soft," and seeking personal comforts and material gains for themselves instead of fighting for the liberation of others. She thinks that the Soviets have abandoned the doctrine of struggle and have adopted the alternative tactics of parliamentary opposition and economic rivalry as a cover for their own laziness or cowardice. She says that the Russians are not even half-revolutionists.

Furthermore, China thinks that the Soviet Union has gone entirely too far in seeking peaceful coexistence with the United States and the rest of the capitalist-imperialist world. China resents the fact that the Soviet Union chooses to discuss nuclear policies and arms control with the United States rather than with her own Communist allies. She chides the Soviet Union for being afraid to wage "just wars," even though the Soviet Union must know that the "East Wind must prevail over the West Wind." China feels that the Soviet Union, by acquiescing ever so slightly in some American overtures for peaceful negotiations in Vietnam, is guilty of conspiring with the United States "to dominate the world." Worst of all, China alleges that Russian nationalism is responsible for shattering the solidarity of the international Communist movement. China thinks that Russian intrigues for a new international Communist conference constitute a nefarious effort to condemn China for heresy and to isolate the Chinese Communists from the rest of the Communist world. After Mao passes from the scene, these official views will be subject to modification.

Communist China regards the United States as its number one enemy, even worse than the Soviet Union. China's first objective in foreign policy is to smash the ring of American bases that encircles China and to drive the American military presence out of East Asia and the Western Pacific. The United States is castigated as the organizer of worldwide military alliances that would wreck or confine China. Chinese leaders blame the United States for blocking the recovery of Taiwan and for seeking to destroy the Chinese Communist system. In Peking, the events of Korea, the offshore islands and Vietnam have been interpreted as one vast crusade against the Chinese Communist regime.

Communist China pours out a steady stream of vitriolic propaganda against the United States as the "leader of the capitalist-imperialist camp." China cannot deny the great tactical strength of the United States, but she insists that "strategically the United States is a paper tiger." China does not doubt that in the long run the schemes of the United States will be defeated by people's wars. In her view, revolution must be all-out revolution, without fear or compromise. Moreover, China's truculence has increased since her demonstration of nuclear capability, which has challenged the Western world's monopoly. Peking contends that American "hawks" and "doves" are equally anti-Chinese, and that most American talk of a new China policy is a vain effort to get out of the blind alley in Vietnam. Chinese propaganda uses the familiar device of distinguishing the "American people" from the nefarious "ruling circles," doubtless intending to promote inner conflict—but this distinction could be useful in later revision of policy. Meanwhile, it is plain that China has shown far more prudence and restraint in action than in words.

She has dabbled in the politics of what she calls the "first intermediate zone," or the underdeveloped areas of Latin America, the Middle

East and Africa. She is determined to be recognized as a truly great power and to have her policies taken into account even in distant lands. She does not have much material help to give, and she cannot match the assistance programs of either the United States or the Soviet Union. Nevertheless, she thinks of herself as the champion of oppressed nations and oppressed peoples, and she offers as much encouragement as she can possibly give to those who are willing to launch their own wars of national liberation. She plays up the themes of anti-imperialism and racial discrimination. She extends diplomatic recognition and gives support to friendly governments, and opposes governments and parties that are well-disposed toward either the United States or the Soviet Union. She vies with the Soviets for the control of local Communist parties. Her record is marred by disappointments, the chief of which have been the failures in Castro's Cuba and the bankruptcy of attempts to form an effective Afro-Asian solidarity organization.

Communist China puts Canada, Great Britain, France, West Germany and others into a category variously known as the "second intermediate zone of advanced Western states" or the "third world." These states, in China's view, are neither fraternal Socialist states nor avowed imperialist enemies. The purposes of Communist China's approaches to the third world are to encourage trade, explore avenues of economic assistance and, if possible, to weaken the influence of the United States and the Soviet Union.

In dealing with Canada, Communist China is aware of the closeness between Canada and the United States, so she proceeds with caution. China has refrained from extreme criticisms of Canadian activities with regard to both Korea and Vietnam which might readily be interpreted as anti-Chinese or pro-American. China has purchased significant amounts of Canadian grain. She has let it be known that she would welcome normalization of relations with Canada on the basis of accepting Peking's position on Taiwan and entry into the United Nations. She treats Australia and New Zealand in much the same way she treats Canada.

Communist China has been more hesitant in dealing with Great Britain than with the other Commonwealth countries. Communist China responded slowly to the British grant of recognition in 1950 and has held up the exchange of full ambassadors. She took offense at British failure to support the seating of Communist China in the United Nations, protested against the treatment of Chinese persons and property in Hong Kong and expressed disapproval of British consular representation in Taipei, Taiwan. Peking placed as many obstacles as possible to the promotion of British trade, perhaps because the British government followed so closely the American line in world affairs. Peking has never forgotten the British record as the arch-imperialist in China and insists that the troubles in Hong Kong will not cease until Hong Kong is again Chinese.

Communist China has achieved better success with France than with Great Britain. China and France see themselves as independent pioneers in the field of nuclear development. Peking has boasted that the Peking-Paris axis is an effective offset to the Washington-London-Moscow combination. Ideological divergencies between China and France are not allowed to get in the way of Machiavellian arrangements in the interest of power politics. Peking and Paris exchanged diplomatic recognition in 1964, and Peking began to view Paris as the great gateway to her rightful place in the society of nations. France and China limited their contacts to polite cooperation, but they supported each other with extravagant propaganda.

Relations with West Germany have been less spectacular than those with France. China is handicapped because of her ideological kinship with East Germany, a fraternal Socialist country. Moreover, West Germany cannot be completely dissociated from the United States. Communist China officially terminated the war against Germany in 1955, and then expanded trade contacts. Peking hopes to find in West Germany, as in Japan, the kind of technical and economic assistance she needs for modernization and industrialization.

Communist China has come to admit that the United Nations is a fact of modern international life that cannot be wished away. Therefore she seeks her "lawful" place in the United Nations on her own terms. In her view, Peking and not Taipei is entitled to every right that the charter assigns to "China."

Peking's past relations with the United Nations have been bitter. She was not only excluded from membership in the world body, but she also felt obliged to fight the entire United Nations in Korea. In 1951 the United Nations passed a resolution condemning Communist China for engaging in aggression, and since that date the majority of member nations has seemed to regard Communist China as the prime disturber of world peace. Naturally, Peking resents this attitude and charges that the United Nations itself is the tool of the United States.

Peking insists on the sole right of representation for China and the definitive expulsion of the "Kuomintang clique." Even if Peking were to be voted to membership, she would accept only on her own conditions. The charter must be reviewed and the United Nations must free itself of American control. The membership must include all "independent" countries and must exclude "American puppets." The United Nations must disavow the wrongful resolutions condemning North Korea and Communist China as aggressors and must pass new resolutions condemning the United States. Peking's attitude is that to her it makes little difference whether or not she joins the United Nations. As stated in the *Peking Review*, "The United States may keep China out of the United Nations for one thousand or even ten thousand years without hurting China one iota. . . . China is doing very well."

The Chinese attitude toward the United Nations illustrates clearly the complexities involved in the establishment and maintenance of world peace. Sovereign nations have their individual and conflicting points of view. China, like those who oppose her, stands by her convictions, and she will not easily be swayed from her chosen course.

The Chinese feel that because of their numbers, the size of their country and their cultural heritage, they are entitled to treatment as one of the great powers. They are confident in their Chinese nationalism and in their Maoist interpretation of international communism. On these premises, they are determined to play a role second to none in world affairs.

5 Christianity in the Life of the Chinese People

Wallace C. Merwin

CHRISTIANITY was present in China as early as the T'ang Dynasty (618-907), in the form of fairly vigorous Nestorian Christian churches. With the decline of the T'ang Dynasty, however, Christianity disappeared except for scattered artifacts and texts.

The Nestorian Church did not reappear in China until the days of the Mongol overrule, which was generally tolerant of all faiths. In the late thirteenth and early fourteenth centuries, Christians were in positions of high authority.

The first Roman Catholic missionary reached China in the late thirteenth century and soon established a modest community. Others followed, but again with the downfall of the Mongol Dynasty, accompanied by strong antiforeign reactions, both Nestorian and Roman Catholic Christianity seem to have completely disappeared.

BEGINNINGS OF THE MODERN MISSIONARY MOVEMENT

With the expansion of European colonialism and trade in the sixteenth and seventeenth centuries and the accompanying activity of the Roman Catholic orders, it was inevitable that Roman Catholic missionaries should again penetrate China. The Jesuits led the way, chiefly through the efforts of the remarkable and brilliant Ricci, who reached Peking in 1601, where he won acceptance as a scholar. For more than a century, Roman Catholic Christianity made considerable headway, continuing through the fall of the Ming Dynasty (1644) and extending into the early years of Manchu rule. Controversy among the Roman Catholic orders over participation by Chinese Christians in Confucian rites culminated in a complete impasse in 1707 between the Papal Legate and the Emperor, and led to the expulsion of many. Severe persecutions of Christians recurred. But by the early nineteenth century the Roman Catholic Church, in spite of great difficulty and persecution, was widely disseminated through the empire, with some native clergy and 200,000 members.

Protestant work began with the arrival of Robert Morrison in 1807, serving under the London Missionary Society. The first American missionaries arrived in Canton in 1830. Early efforts were chiefly under the auspices of the American

Board of Commissioners for Foreign Missions, but Baptists, Episcopalians and Presbyterians soon followed. In time, Protestant missionaries from many lands, representing every variety of Protestant belief and practice, entered China; so that, along with that of the Roman Catholics, this came to be one of the largest organized missionary efforts in history. By 1925, the peak of missionary personnel, there were 4,492 Protestant missionaries in China from Canada and the United States and 3,171 from other parts of the world.

The difficulties facing the Christian mission to China were formidable. The missionaries came out of an almost totally different culture and often had little understanding of Chinese history or culture. The cultural differences were most severe in the early period, though even among the early missionaries there were men of great understanding and ability who became genuine scholars of things Chinese. With all its weaknesses and fissions, China still represented an ancient and highly developed culture. The population and territory were so great that the missionary movement even at its height touched hardly more than a small fraction. There was general suspicion of outsiders and of non-Chinese concepts. Opposition, especially before the fall of the empire (1911), was chiefly led by the Confucian gentry, the backbone of the increasingly inflexible and outmoded structure of Chinese society. They resented alien intrusion, saw their own power threatened, particularly by Western educational concepts that challenged the Confucian classics, and resented the missionaries' work among the illiterate and dispossessed. The republican revolution realized the inadequacies of China's traditional educational and governmental structure, but growing nationalism increased antiforeign resentments. This was sharply true of the extreme nationalism of the 1920's and later, and most of all of the rise of the Communist movement, with its strong antireligious bias. The materialism that is strong in Chinese character was also enhanced by the scientism and skepticism of much of the modern education that was introduced from Japan and the West.

Inevitably, association of the missionaries with Western imperialism and exploitation, even where the missionary sought to repudiate such connections, made difficulty. Missionaries were nationals of the Western powers. Their very presence was made possible by virtue of what the Chinese universally considered Unequal Treaties. The pressure of the Western powers for what they felt was normal freedom for their nationals to trade and live in China forced upon the empire, notably after the armed conflict with England and France in 1858-1860, treaties that opened the interior to trade and missionary effort. Western governments sometimes used incidents involving missionaries to bring pressure on the Chinese for enforcement of these treaties.

One significant instance of territorial aggrandizement, long planned in the rivalry of international politics, was the German seizure of Kiaochow (Tsingtao) in 1898, which used the murder of missionaries as a pretext for action.

The Western missionary was accustomed to a different standard of living than most Chinese, was much better paid and usually lived in conspicuous, though by Western standards unpretentious, houses. Especially in the early years, the missionary, the church and its institutions (and sometimes a number of Chinese converts) were grouped in walled compounds, to some degree set off from Chinese society as an exclusive and privileged group. The church and its institutions were Western in character and often in physical appearance. In spite of emphasis on self-support and the development of an indigenous church, missionaries were often reluctant to relinquish control. Potential Chinese leadership was alienated by such factors. Some of the Chinese who did come into leadership were more Western (modern) in their education and outlook than they were Chinese (traditional).

There were also many factors favorable to the advancement of the Christian cause. With the decline of the empire came great disillusionment with the Manchu regime and the humiliating defeats caused by its increasing sterility and unwillingness to accept new ways and modern learning. There was increasing intellectual ferment and avid interest in Western education.

Strong republican sympathy identified democracy and hopes for the renewal of the nation with Western ideals. A number of national leaders in the Republican period were at least nominally Christian, notably Sun Yat-sen and Chiang Kai-shek. Neither was an active churchman and their apprehension of the fullness of Christian faith may be open to question, but the very fact of their profession of Christianity provided some measure of protection and encouragement to Christians. The crumbling of authority in the early twentieth century, with a strong desire to find an alternative to the old ways, was also favorable to the Christian cause.

Chinese Churches in the Twentieth Century

The first half of the twentieth century was a period of remarkable development in the Protestant Christian movement, characterized by the increase of churches and other institutions. Church members increased from about 100,000 in 1900 to approximately 400,000 by 1921, a growth of 300 percent. In the next sixteen years there was a further increase of 50 percent. More than 200,000 were then added in the troubled and disruptive period leading up to the change in political regime in 1949. This growth was paralleled by a steady increase in the numbers and quality of Chinese workers, who by 1920 numbered 28,000, about equally divided between church and institutional work. By this time, ordained Chinese outnumbered missionaries in the same category, a numerical superiority that steadily increased.

One striking example of the growth in Chinese leadership is the fact that in the 1907 conference to celebrate the Centennial of Protestant mission work in China, only nine Chinese were present among 1,000 missionaries. By 1922, when a truly national Christian Conference met in Shanghai, Chinese outnumbered missionaries. All major addresses and reports were in Chinese, and the chairman was a Chinese clergyman. One of the decisions of this Conference was the establishment of the National Christian Council of China. By 1950, at a meeting of the National Christian Council there were no foreign missionaries present.

Church leaders of high character and marked ability emerged. One of the most notable was C. Y. Cheng (Ch'eng Ching-yi), a forceful speaker and able administrator prominent in the National Christian Council and in the Church of Christ in China. Two churchmen identified with Yenching University School of Religion (Peking) influenced Christian thinking: T. T. Lew, educator, editor and hymn writer; and T. C. Chao, China's most prominent theologian, a writer of distinctively Chinese hymns and a President of the World Council of Churches. In the Anglican-Episcopal Church, a group of able leaders emerged as bishops, typified by Robin Chen (Ch'en Chien-chen), Presiding

Bishop, and T. K. Shen (Shen Tzu-kao), an administrator and theological educator. Similarly in the Methodist Church, the two active Chinese bishops during the 1940's represented the able leadership that had come to the fore in China: W. Y. Chen (Ch'en Wen-yuan), the wartime General Secretary of the National Christian Council of China, was a vigorous and able administrator who experienced some years of imprisonment after the Communists came to power. Z. T. Kaung (Chiang Ch'ang-ch'uan), an outstanding pastor, baptized Generalissimo Chiang Kai-shek.

Not less significant was the high quality of Christian lay leadership, which played an important part in the development of the nation as well as of the church. Many of China's doctors were Christians or educated in Christian schools, and the schools of nursing connected with Christian hospitals and medical colleges trained a remarkably high percentage of the nation's nurses. Men such as Dr. F. C. Yen, long associated with Yale-in-China's medical work, played a major part in the development of modern medicine in China through stimulation of official interest in improving health standards, the development of medical institutions and the promotion of public health training. Three of the five Chinese delegates to the Versailles Peace Conference following World War I were Christians. The Young Men's Christian Association, essentially a lay movement, produced many leaders of note, among them David Z. T. Yui, a General Secretary of the YMCA as well as Chairman of the National Christian Council; C. T. Wang, also a YMCA General Secretary and later a prominent political figure who served as Foreign Minister for some years. It was an ironic fact that Protestant Christianity produced many national leaders of note but was weak in leadership at the local level.

A notable factor in the slow and difficult expansion in the interior was the work of the China Inland Mission, pioneer and norm of nondenominational "faith" missions. With increasing freedom of movement and growing acceptance of foreigners, many missionaries found their way even to the smaller towns of remote provinces.

While this summary deals primarily with the Protestant Church in China, brief mention should be made of the extensive Roman Catholic work in the twentieth century, similar in significant problems and achievements. There was great growth in membership, from 750,000 in 1900 to about 3,300,000 in 1940. The development of Roman Catholic educational and medical institutions in general was later and not so extensive on the upper levels as that of the Protestants; the Catholics put greater emphasis on primary schools and on simple dispensaries.

There was a marked increase in missionary personnel as well as in Chinese leadership. The number of women workers increased greatly, and there were 5,000 Chinese sisters by 1948.

CHRISTIANITY IN CHINESE LIFE

The percentage of ordained men in total workers, both foreign and Chinese, was considerably higher among the Catholics than among the Protestants. The first Chinese bishops were consecrated in 1926. The appointment in 1946 of the first Chinese cardinal marked the recognition of a Roman Catholic Church of China directly under the Pope and no longer under the missionary orders or the Propaganda. As the era of Communist rule began, however, with its severe restrictions, there were still more foreign priests than Chinese, and approximately 80 percent of the bishops were missionaries.

An important element in Roman Catholic work since 1920 was the increasing number of American missionaries. Catholic work had previously been conducted by the European orders and congregations, particularly the French. The Americans often brought a fresh outlook from a multireligious society, with emphasis on activism and freedom within tradition. The chief American units at work in China have been the Maryknoll Mission (The Catholic Foreign Mission Society of America, Inc.), the Jesuits (California Province) and the Society of the Divine Word (American section).

THE CHURCH IN SERVICE

Many Christian schools in China originated in the nineteenth century as primary schools. In the early part of the twentieth century, with the general growth of education and rise in standards, junior and senior middle schools evolved and then, principally after 1900, institutions of college and university grade. In the early years, it was the Christian schools that introduced such revolutionary ideas as the education of women, the concept of universal education and the pragmatic emphasis on education for all the tasks of society rather than for an élite of scholar-officials. These schools were generally characterized by high educational and moral standards, which often led non-Christians, including many of wealth and high position, to send their children to them.

The early Christian schools had produced most of the leadership of the church, a natural result when the Christian community was small and a person's very enrollment in one of the schools symbolized a break with Chinese tradition. In later years, though the number of students was vastly greater and Western education generally popular, it was inevitable that those who went into Christian work were fewer numerically and proportionately. Moreover, even those students who had a valid Christian experience in school found it difficult to adjust to the life of the local congregation, often led by pastors less well trained than themselves. Many never identified themselves with local churches, but did carry into commercial life or government service an enlightened Christian conscience and a deep concern for their own people.

An important element in the remarkable growth of Christian schools, especially at university level, was the coming into prominence of men and women of high Christian character and considerable influence in Chinese society. Examples are President Herman C. E. Liu of the University of Shanghai, Dean T. H. Sun of Cheeloo University, President Wu Yi-fang of Ginling College, President Y. C. Yang of Soochow University and Professor P. C. Hsu of Yenching University. These and others like them were notable not only as educators but as active church men and women and as public figures of considerable influence.

By 1936, the year before the major Japanese invasion, which did much to stem the strong tide of progress of the early 1930's in China and closed many of the Christian schools and other institutions, there were 13 Protestant colleges or universities with more than 15,000 graduates, 269 middle schools and approximately 3,000 primary schools. The influence of this large educational program on the modernization of China was considerable.

The missionaries recognized from the first the necessity for training Chinese leadership. Gradually, theological seminaries evolved in many areas, most of them interdenominational. The most notable in the recent history of the church in China were Union Theological Seminary, Canton; Yenching University School of Religion, Peking; Nanking Theological Seminary; Central

Theological School (Anglican-Episcopal), Nanking and Shanghai; West China Theological Seminary, Chengtu; and the North China Theological Seminary (Presbyterian), T'eng-hsien. A survey of Protestant theological education led by Dean Luther Weigle of Yale Divinity School in 1935, *Education for Service in the Christian Church in China,* reported on 13 institutions of college level (most of them interdenominational) and 15 schools of senior high school grade.

Early clinics grew into hospitals of far-reaching influence and service, in a period when the great mass of the Chinese people had no medical service except that of the traditional herbalists. The growth of the nursing profession was likewise largely due to the training program of the Christian hospitals. C. P. Fitzgerald, the Australian historian of China, says, "The whole Chinese medical profession owes its origin to their [the missionaries'] teaching."

By 1936 there were 232 Protestant Christian hospitals and branches in China, the majority in small cities where they provided virtually the only modern medical facilities. No less important was the contribution made by such Christian medical schools as Cheeloo University (Tsinan), St. John's University (Shanghai), Hackett Memorial Medical College (Canton), West China Union Medical College (Chengtu) and Mukden Medical College. Moreover, the base for the secular Peking Union Medical College, outstanding in all the Far East, was a Christian medical college formed by the major missions in Peking early in the twentieth century.

The effectiveness of the hospitals in evangelism was notable. Service to mankind without ulterior motive is a valid and essential Christian witness, growing out of Christian love and concern. But the compassion, kindliness and concern for individuals, as well as good medical standards, found in Christian hospitals, staffed largely by devoted Chinese Christians, brought many who passed through their doors into an understanding of vital, active Christian faith.

Everywhere the Christian missionary has gone he has encouraged literacy and developed Christian publications, partly from conviction of the necessity for Christians to be able to read the Bible and have adequate interpretation of Christian teaching. Christian books in Chinese were very early prepared by Protestant missionaries, and a number of missions developed presses (of which the most notable was the American Presbyterian Mission Press). Timothy Richard, British missionary of the late nineteenth century, had a vision of a China illuminated by the best of Western learning and was a chief agent in the development of the interdenominational Christian Literature Society for China. By World War I, there had developed what was in Latourette's judgment "a Christian literature which was probably richer and more varied than that produced by Protestant missionaries in any other language." A considerable volume of Christian literature was produced, including not only basic books for the new Christian, hymnals and commentaries, but theological works and serious approaches to the great issues of the day. Many were works or translations by missionaries, but an increasing number of writers were Chinese. It was also significant that a number of Chinese Christian publishing ventures entered the field and that in the development of some major secular companies Chinese Christians had an important role.

The Bible societies were active from an early period, translating and publishing the Scriptures in various styles and vernaculars, the most successful, still largely in use, being the Mandarin or Union Version completed in 1920. This achievement was of great help to the linguistic revolution that led the way in the substitution of the colloquial for the archaic classical language, of incalculable importance for the spread of modern education. It no doubt accounted in part for the amazing numbers of Bible portions and New Testaments sold.

The annual reports of the Bible societies show that from a circulation of about 2,500,000 items in 1905, there was an increase to more than 6,000,000 in 1914. Each year from 1932 to 1936 about 9,000,000 portions were distributed, and more than 76,000 whole Bibles and 87,000 New Testaments were sold in 1936. The war years brought a sharp decline in the number of portions, though the total of New Testaments exceeded 111,000 in 1939 and again in 1948, while in 1939 123,068 full Bibles were sold. Such figures indicate interest far outside the church membership of less than a million.

Christian compassion and concern also found expression in leprosaria, schools for the blind, deaf and dumb, and child welfare agencies—fields of service pioneered almost entirely by Christians. Efforts to improve the lot of the poverty-stricken masses led to the establishment of social welfare programs such as the Moore Memorial Institute and the South Gate Social Center in Shanghai, while countless self-help and handicraft projects sprang up, with varying degrees of success. Efforts to help the farmer to be more productive led to a number of rural improvement programs such as the North China Rural Service Union, with field programs in horticulture, agronomy and animal husbandry. Thousands of farmers were trained in short-term institutes, and better seeds and improved breeds of livestock and poultry were introduced, bringing large-scale benefits to farmers.

Christian universities pioneered in community development enterprises, notably through the University of Nanking Rural Reconstruction Program and similar programs operated by Yenching and Cheeloo Universities. These included educational efforts for farmers, development of credit unions, the organization of marketing associations and rural health programs. Some of the earliest work in agricultural science was done through the University of Nanking's College of Agriculture and Forestry, established in 1913. Not to be forgotten are the large-scale efforts to minister to emergency needs, in which Christian forces played a major part. These often provided the only hope for survival, notably during the terrible drought and famine in the Northwest in the early 1920's, the floods of 1931 in Central China and 1939 in North China and the unprecedented dislocation of vast segments of the population in the years following the Japanese invasion of 1937.

The Christian Community in 1950

By 1949-1950, when the Communists won complete control and established the People's Republic of China, there were about 1,000,000 baptized members of all of the Protestant churches, while Roman Catholics numbered approximately 3,000,000. Christianity exercised a much greater influence on Chinese society than this modest count would indicate, particularly through its educational and medical institutions and its enlightened, well-trained and socially conscious leadership in many areas of secular life.

Surveying the China scene today, the efforts of the Protestant missionary movement resulted in apparent failure, and yet the missionaries unquestionably left a mark. Whatever their shortcomings and inner motivations, in hospitals, schools, and chapels they stood forth as men who believed in the sacredness of human personality. For one hundred years, men of goodwill dedicated their lives to giving to the Chinese an understanding of the Christian view of life and of Christian values. While only a very small percentage of Chinese came to understand them, it would be rash to conclude that the values they endeavored to foster have been forgotten.[1]

The very magnitude of the Christian witness to China inevitably reflected the divisions of the church in the West. The *Directory of the Protestant Christian Movement in China* (1950) reported more than thirty denominational church bodies, aided or supplemented by a hundred mission societies. This variety stemmed in part from the fact that Protestant Christian work was carried on in China by representatives from approximately twenty countries. On the other hand, the numerical strength of the church was concentrated largely in the major denominational bodies, perhaps two-thirds being found in the Church of Christ in China, Methodist, Anglican-Episcopal, Lutheran, Baptist and other groupings derived from "historic" churches.

The divisions in the church were not only denominational but also, as in the West, derived from the various degrees of theological and social conservatism and liberalism that divided both missionaries and Chinese leaders. Such variety was further extended by the growth of a number of indigenous Chinese groups, some of which were highly emotional.

Furthermore, it is important to remember that

the church, like the nation, had suffered staggering blows through the years of the war with Japan (1937-1945, but affecting an important segment in Manchuria from 1931) and by the years of civil war that followed. Mortality among church members and leaders was heavy, and there was a serious hiatus in theological education. Factionalism and regionalism, common in Chinese society, also found their expression in the church.

Still, there was a high degree of effective cooperation and unity among the historic churches, most notably in institutional work. Indeed, it seems that more unity and cooperation was achieved among Protestant groups than among the Roman Catholic orders, in spite of the monolithic image of the Roman Catholic Church. Most of the institutions of higher education were interdenominational. Major mission bodies traditionally operated under comity agreements, so that geographically they supplemented one another, instead of competing. Through such agencies as the National Christian Council of China, the China Christian Educational Association, the Christian Medical Council, the China Sunday School Union and the National Committee for Christian Religious Education, the major Protestant bodies worked together at the national level. The Church of Christ in China, the largest Protestant church body, brought together most Congregational and Presbyterian work, as well as some Baptists, the Evangelical

United Brethren, the Evangelical and Reformed Church, the United Church of Canada and others. In the Sheng Kung Hui (Holy Catholic Church) was merged the Anglican-Episcopal work of many societies, while most of the Lutherans were eventually organized into a single Chinese church body.

CHRISTIANITY UNDER COMMUNIST RULE

After the Communist regime came to power (1949), it soon became apparent that the activities of the church would be severely circumscribed.[2] Service institutions were quickly taken over by the state. Many Protestant missionaries left as the Communists drove down to the South and on to the West, though in 1949-1950 about 1,000 were still in China. Those who remained found themselves restricted in their movements and activities and increasingly an embarrassment to the church. Consequently, most withdrew, particularly after the beginning of the Korean War in mid-1950, when the anti-American campaign became violent and pressures on missionaries of all nationalities increased. Some were placed under house arrest; a limited number were imprisoned, usually for short periods but a few for extensive terms. More of the Roman Catholic missionaries, obedient to ecclesiastical authority, courageously attempted to stay, and many of them were able to do so until 1952 or 1953. In the span from 1945 to 1953, a number were killed by the Communists, more were imprisoned, while hundreds of Chinese priests suffered like fates, many of them still remaining in prison.

The rural churches, many of which had already been closed in areas controlled by the Communists, were for the most part shut down during the period of land reform. A few of them reopened later, but church activities were generally restricted to Sunday worship services in the cities. In 1958, after the counterattacks following the free speaking of the "Hundred Flowers" period (when some church and cultural leaders spoke out critically), the number of churches declined sharply and a good deal of church property was "voluntarily" turned over to the state. In the smaller cities, usually only one church remained open. In Shanghai, where there had been approximately two hundred Protestant churches, only about twenty could continue —a number soon reduced even further. Pastors and other church workers were forced into thoroughgoing study groups, which urgently pressed Marxist teachings and required confession of past mistakes and changes in thinking. Most church workers were compelled to engage in "productive labor." The management of former mission property was assumed by a state agency, and in some cases the much-reduced income of the churches was supplemented by grants to those churches that cooperated with the regime and enjoyed its favor.

Theological education declined. Most of the

former institutions at various grades were merged into four. In 1956, Bishop Rajah B. Manikam of India reported four theological schools then open, with a total of 398 students. By 1965, only one institution was open, with about 85 students, obviously not enough to supply even a decimated church. There appears to have been a serious decline in the number of church members, even though there were fairly numerous accessions and some new church buildings in the early part of this period. Visitors to China have rather consistently been told, both by church leaders and government officials, that there were about 700,000 Protestants in China, a reduction of 200,000 or more from the number in 1949.

The official policy of the government has been one of "freedom of religion," incorporated in an article in the Constitution. (The Chinese term used, however, is literally translated as "freedom to believe," which is narrower in scope.) There is no broad guarantee of freedom of association or publication, and it was specifically stated on occasion that this policy did not mean freedom to evangelize. It was also specified that there was freedom to oppose religious belief—a freedom implemented by severe restrictions on religious activity and by massive public teaching and propaganda against religion. In general, the leadership of the church enthusiastically endorsed the new government and its programs without accepting the whole of its Marxist ideology. Visitors to China were informed that the government had been generous in its treatment of the church. Most of the vocal leaders took a strongly nationalistic position and were highly critical of ecumenical Protestant bodies. They categorized missionary activity of the past as reactionary and imperialistic, and ties with all outside churches were severed. Denominational lines lost meaning, though there seemed to be no movement toward organized church union.

The only active and recognized church agency was "The Chinese Christian Three-Self Movement" (utilizing the traditional missionary slogans of self-government, self-support and self-propagation), loosely organized at local as well as national levels. It seems to have been not only a device to encourage cooperation with the government, but also one accepted by some Christian leaders as a protection for the Protestant Christian forces.

With the Cultural Revolution, a new era began. The Red Guards first appeared in the summer of 1966. Fanatical bands of young students, many of them teen-agers, fiercely attacked everything and everyone with ties to the past or to the West in their officially sanctioned crusade against the "four olds" (old culture, old thinking, old habits, old customs). Many Christians and others had their homes ransacked and possessions destroyed, and suffered cruel personal indignities. The churches were generally vandalized. Hymn books and Bibles were burned, religious symbols destroyed or defaced, church buildings taken over as dormitories or warehouses. So far as is known at this writing, there is virtually no public religious observance in China.

How did the Chinese people respond to the Christian mission? In terms of numbers, the response was small in relation to the enormous population. In determining the course of the nation's development, and in total impact on Chinese society and such massive problems as hunger, poverty and overpopulation, the measurable results were slight. On the other hand, the contributions of Christians to the Chinese nation in education and medicine, and in the concepts of the worth of every person, of social consciousness and responsibility and of the brotherhood of man, were not insignificant. The fact that a surprising number of the ablest and most responsible leaders of the nation in the 1920-1950 period, in both public and private life, were Christians, and an even larger number educated in Christian schools, certainly gave evidence of a vital contribution to Chinese life. While only a limited range of the Chinese people was touched by the work of the Christian church as church, the number who found physical healing and more abundant life through faith in God and the service of man was impressive.

The Christian church and its institutions introduced many Chinese to free debate and democratic procedures. Ordained Chinese pastors were greatly outnumbered by lay workers in all facets of church life. This is not unrelated to Chinese respect for education and medicine and to the popular concept of the professional religious worker as a parasite or recluse. Moreover, Chinese activism was reinforced and abetted by such tendencies in the Western missionary community.

In assessing the contributions of Christianity to Chinese society, we cannot forget the tremendous influence of Christians in combating such major evils as the opium traffic and footbinding, in elevating the status of women and in recognizing the worth and potential of the handicapped, who were rejected by traditional Chinese society. Much of the impact of Christianity in China came through individuals whose lives had been touched and changed by the Christian faith. Through its teachings, many Chinese found new meaning and hope in spite of the despair so common in the chaotic years of the twentieth century. The contribution of Christians to the relief of suffering in times of emergency was especially significant. *The China Critic*, an independent English language Chinese weekly, said in an editorial during the war years:

One of the many things that have come out of the present has been the realization that, whatever doubt may have existed in the past, the Christian missions in China fully and indisputably justify their existence. . . . They have preached the gospel not with

CHRISTIANITY IN CHINESE LIFE 141

words but by a practical demonstration of the love of God and the brotherhood of man.[3]

What about the future? Will Christianity disappear again in China as it did on two previous occasions? Or with the certainty of change in China, will public worship and a visible church come to the surface again? Most of those who were leaders of the church when the great changes of 1949-1950 took place are aged, out of touch with the church and its development elsewhere and out of favor with the secular powers in China. Even the limited able younger leadership that has arisen in recent years is now submerged, and the meager theological training facilities are no longer functioning. It is clear that the future of Christianity in China now depends not on the organized church but on the faithfulness and witness of individual Christians.

It is not possible for us to say what the final outcome will be. We can only leave such matters in the hands of God and of the Christian people of China, who have demonstrated their faithfulness in the past. Meanwhile, it is surely our Christian responsibility to seek to understand the situation in which Chinese Christians live and to be ready to meet them in Christian fellowship when opportunity offers.

Professor Kenneth Scott Latourette, for decades a leading authority on China, has written of the whole process of change in the twentieth century:

Here is a spectacle the like of which in sheer magnitude human beings have never before seen. The largest fairly homogeneous group of mankind is experiencing the most thoroughgoing revolution in its history. . . . There is every indication that the full outcome will not be clearly discerned for at least a generation and probably very much longer. . . . The world should not lose faith in China even if the process requires centuries. Many of us who have loved the Chinese have a hopeful confidence in the ultimate result and base it upon what we know of Chinese history and of individual Chinese of today. Remembering as we do the ability which the Chinese have shown in the past to construct a civilization, we believe that they will . . . once more create a worthy culture.[4]

Footnotes

1. Paul A. Varg, *Missionaries, Chinese, and Diplomats; the American Protestant Missionary Movement in China, 1890-1952*. Princeton: Princeton University Press, 1958, pp. 324-325.

2. Francis P. Jones, *The Church in Communist China*. New York: Friendship Press, 1962. A careful account and interpretation of the Protestant experience.

3. *The China Critic*, July 20, 1939, p. 36.

4. Kenneth S. Latourette, *The Chinese, Their History and Culture*. New York: Macmillan, 1964, pp. 680-681.